PRAISE FOR

Promises Broken

Mission-driven work has never been more important—or more demanding. This book is an essential read for anyone who has poured their heart into a cause, only to find themselves struggling within unhealthy organizational cultures. It unpacks the underlying patterns that can make purpose-driven work unsustainable, equipping readers with the awareness to identify and navigate unhealthy dynamics.

This book is an invaluable guide for anyone committed to making an impact—without losing themselves in the process.

~ **Anu Malipatil**, Executive Director
Overdeck Family Foundation

PROMISES BROKEN

Reclaiming Your Health and Humanity When Mission-Driven Work Lets You Down

Susan Beth Cocuzza

Disclaimer

The information in this book is based on the author's knowledge, experience, and opinions. The information provided is for general informational purposes only. The author is not a licensed healthcare provider and the content of this book is based on personal experiences and reflections. This book is not intended as a substitute for the advice of a licensed mental health practitioner. Should the reader be experiencing workplace abuse, elevated levels of stress, anxiety, or depression, or other mental health concerns, it strongly recommended that a therapist or other mental health provider be consulted. The author and publisher assume no responsibility for any actions taken based on the information presented in this book.

All names and identifying details throughout this book have been changed to protect the privacy of the individuals who were interviewed. The places of employment in these stories are a creation of the author's imagination. Any similarity to a real place of employment is purely coincidental.

# Contents

Introduction	**1**
Companion Journal Available for Download	9
Part I: The Promise	**11**
Chapter 1: Mission-Drive Work	13
Chapter 2: Meet Our Friends	25
Part II: Discovering a Harsh Reality	**47**
Chapter 3: Toxic Work Culture Defined	49
Chapter 4: Miah's Efforts Are Thwarted	71
Chapter 5: Briana's Honeymoon Is Over	83
Chapter 6: Evelyn's Heroes Fall From Greatness	93
Chapter 7: Nina's Kindness Is Not Reciprocated	101
Chapter 8: Faith's Rocky Hike to the Glass Cliff	111
Part III: Hitting Rock Bottom	**123**
Chapter 9: Toughing It Out	125
Chapter 10: Our Friends Hit Rock Bottom	135
Part IV: Finding Inspiration	**155**
Chapter 11: Our Friends Find a Path Forward	157
Chapter 12: Finding Your Path	167
Author's Note	183
Epilogue	**185**
Advice From Our Friends	187
Final Words From the Author	197
Notes & References	201
Acknowledgements	205
About the Author	207

For Mel, thank you.

Introduction

"When the whole world is silent, even one voice becomes powerful."

— Malala Yousafzai

Working for a mission-driven organization should be life-giv-ing—*and it can completely drain the life out of you.*

You can love the work you are meant to do—*and hate your job.*

You can care about the kids (or clients, or patients)—*at the expense of caring for yourself.*

Unfortunately, these contradictions are not only the reality but are also pervasive in nonprofit and mission-driven work. And they shouldn't be. We hear about toxic work culture in corporate work environments, and perhaps we've come to expect it there. When profit is the bottom line, it's easy to excuse poor behavior. (We shouldn't, but that's a topic for another book.) But when the work is centered on a mission, its purpose being to make the world a better place, we expect our workplaces to be immune from this toxicity.

Aah, but they are not. Many employees in mission-driven work-places share the same experience.

We start out full of optimism, passion, and enthusiasm that fuels our day to day. We come into this work because of the mission. It's not a mistake that we work there. We believe in what the organization sets out to do, and we know that every individual contributes to achieving the organization's vision.

And not long after we start, the sparkle begins to fade as reality hits. We may see that while the visionary leader of the organization has amazing ideas, they have weak leadership skills and use micromanagement and bullying to drive the work. We may learn that there is an aversion to change or a lack of trust at the organization, creating a culture of fear and secrecy. We may learn that premature growth has created a lack of clarity around the theory of change and there is no cohesion across the organization. We may find ourselves on a dysfunctional team or in the midst of a relationship with a challenging boss. The shiny gleam of optimism is gone, and over time, we become demoralized and frustrated, or even physically sick.

I know because it happened to me.

In early June 2023, I facilitated the second day of a two-day meeting from the floor of a conference room. I had debilitating back pain that made it impossible for me to walk, stand, or sit in one position for more than five minutes at a time. The pain had started eight months prior and gradually grew in intensity over time. During that period, I continued to commute three days a week, two hours each direction, because my boss was easier to work with in person. My peers and my manager would ask periodically what I was doing to take care of the pain, saying,

"You should really take care of that," but the culture was not accepting of anything less than my best. So, to avoid the disappointment of letting people down, I kept pushing.

Laying on the floor of the conference room that day, I came to the somewhat obvious conclusion that I had finally hit rock bottom. I left the meeting and went straight to a doctor. (But not until after I had walked all over the two-floor office to be sure my unfinished work was handed off to responsible people before leaving.) Within 36 hours of leaving and being told I had let my boss down by "not having everything taken care of," I was in emergency surgery for a complete L4-L5 herniation that was pressing dangerously on my nerve column. Given the amount of IV pain medication I was on, I still can't fathom how I had been walking around as the host of a meeting and a team dinner two days before.

Six weeks of medical leave for my recovery was the gift I needed for a serious awakening. I came to realize that this job, the culture of the organization, and the unrelenting expectations of my boss were doing some tremendous harm. To me and to my family. My oldest child had graduated from high school the week before I went to the ER and was about to head off to college. My marriage was suffering. And I will never forget the line my younger son wrote in his high school English paper: "For the last two years, my mom worked 24/7 at a job that didn't appreciate her at all." They all saw the choices I was making, and it wasn't okay.

As I finished my medical leave, I made the decision to resign. Three days after returning to work, I handed in my notice. I quit, even with college tuition bills on the horizon and no immediate plan other than recovery. During this time, I started watching and listening and reading, trying to figure out what went wrong. I read memoirs, listened to podcasts, and followed new people on social media. I quickly realized I was not alone. I learned that so many women feel stuck doing "good work" that is not good for them. So many are told that leaving is weak, that they would be giving up on "the kids" or "the client" or "the mission." That if they leave, it means they failed: they couldn't successfully balance work and motherhood.

But I noticed something else, something powerful. When these women found each other, when one person could identify with someone else's story and put words to their own experience, they found a community. They found validation for their own experiences. And they found strength to make a change.

At this point, I knew what I had to do.

I founded my business, Almavina Strategic Partners, and started a movement to create people-first workplaces—ones in which people look forward to going to work. I decided that it was time to call attention to what was happening behind closed doors and to make mission-driven work not only a place where good work is done, but also a place where the people doing the work can thrive. To this end, I work with organizational leadership and individuals who want to make a difference, because that's the way we make change: one organization, one person at a time.

In addition, I decided that stories like mine had to be told. It's time for real talk about work culture, because that's how we build community and begin to fix a broken system.

Promises Broken aims to expand upon the validation and community those initial books, posts, podcasts, and new connections offered me. It aims to provide another source of evidence that you are not alone. To give you the language to describe what you are experiencing. To build a community, even if you don't know everyone personally. One that gives you the strength to seek more, that helps you believe you deserve better, whether that means bravely leaving or speaking up and making changes in the workplace.

In this book, I will take you on a journey of what it's like to work in a mission-driven organization with a toxic culture—from the optimism and hope at the outset, through the confusing reality, and to rock bottom. I will introduce you to five friends, real women who worked across different sectors in mission-driven spaces. Real women who experienced toxic workplaces and suffered personal consequences from it. We will follow them on their individual journeys as we learn about the unique aspects of mission-driven work that make these organizations a perfect backdrop for toxic culture and mistreatment.

But don't despair—this is not a "burn book" that aims to simply document all the horrible things that have happened. At the end, as I share the conclusion of our friends' stories, we will return to our sense of hope and optimism. Because together we will see there is hope. Our friends want you to hear their stories so you, too, can find validation, community, strength, and inspiration.

Whether you are experiencing something similar at your work, someone you love is navigating this challenge, or even if it's not happening to you yet but you see the potential for it to happen at your workplace, this book is for you. May it inspire you to make a change, seek more, and prioritize health and humanity for yourself, your colleagues, and all the people you care about.

# Companion Journal Available For Download

To download the companion journal for *Promises Broken*, go to www.almavina.com/PBjournal.

While simply reading this book all the way through will deliver immense value, the companion journal includes content designed to take your reflections a step further.

As the journal provides prompts and exercises not found in the book, it's best used in parallel with your first read, containing prompts applicable to each chapter to deepen your personal reflection. It can also be used as a way to reengage with the content after you have finished the book.

If you choose to use the journal as you read, you will notice prompts like the one below throughout the text to indicate an ideal moment for reflection. Let's get started!

 After downloading the journal, spend a moment with the Introduction prompts for a guided reflection before you begin Chapter 1.

PART I
The Promise

"Optimism is a strategy for making a better future. Because unless you believe that the future can be better, you are unlikely to step up and take responsibility for making it so."

— Noam Chomsky

Mission-Driven Work

Mission-driven work is full of promise; promise for a fulfilling career, promise for a better future, promise that your days will contribute to a greater good. But as easily as promises are made, they can also be broken.

Anecdotal evidence tells us that people are drawn to mission-driven work because they care deeply about a cause. There is a sense of optimism, a promise for a better future. They believe in the mission of the organization—there might even be a personal connection to it. They believe they are joining a team of people who collectively believe in that mission. The work itself is rewarding and meaningful for everyone involved.

To support these claims, the following statements were found on various nonprofit organizations' "Meet the Team" web pages within the bios of people working across industries. One can feel their sense of optimism and their personal connection to their work.

In 2007 an ad for St. Jude's stating "be thankful for the healthy children in your life and give to those who are not" hit home after a brief leukemia possibility tied to another diagnosis arose with her youngest child. The opportunity to work with [the organization] arose; she has been involved ever since.

[Name] joined [this organization] to be a part of a team committed to serving students who have been historically and systemically underserved by our country's education system. She believes in the power of all students to succeed, without exception, when given the necessary tools and support to thrive as their authentic selves.

She is a committed and passionate music education advocate and has spent her career working directly with students, families, educators and communities to improve and expand accessibility for individuals to engage with art in meaningful ways and use it as a catalyst for social change.

Promises Broken leads us through a journey that is all too common in mission-driven work. It starts with passion and optimism—that feeling of deep commitment to a cause and the promise of having a positive impact on the world.

Next comes an unfortunate reality—the possibility that, despite the goodness of the cause, the workplace might not be a healthy and supportive environment. The fact that the work is good work does not on its own mean the organization has a strong and positive culture or that the "good" is found within the company as well as in the work it does. These difficult work environments can have a significant impact on the health and well-being of employees, especially those who came to the work with a strong and genuine connection to the mission. For those, this reality can be devastating.

And yet, there is hope. Even after hitting rock bottom (and hopefully before!), employees who have been demoralized on this journey can address their suffering and reclaim their passion for the work that they love.

You might be wondering, is this the guaranteed path for every mission-driven workplace? Absolutely not. But it is, unfortunately, more common than it should be. The general consensus and expectation is that corporate culture = bad, while nonprofit culture = good. And in support of this theory, we have heard many stories of poor corporate culture. Stories of women experiencing gender discrimination and harassment. Stories of workplace bullying that get swept under the rug to protect the bully. Stories of victim payouts that include legally binding non-disclosure agreements so the truth of the toxic culture can't be revealed.

But what if that kind of culture existed in the places where "good" work is happening as well?

Spoiler alert: it does.

Because even when the entire organization is committed to changing the world for the better, individuals can still show up in terrible ways. Leaders still jump into leading without the skills they need to do so effectively. They might mean well, but they don't know how to get the job done and instead end up building an organization that is destined for toxicity. People with outsized egos and narcissistic personalities still exist in these organizations, and they can do tremendous damage to organizational culture.

So, no, mission-driven work is not immune to toxic work culture, and it's a problem that needs to be addressed.

What Is Mission-Driven Work?

Before we go further, let's get clear on what we mean by "mission-driven work." Today, many companies across industries would consider themselves "mission-driven," because they have a company mission that guides their work. There is a growing trend in business to anchor work in a mission—and that is a good practice! A mission keeps the team aligned on what they are trying to achieve. And, many of those companies are also trying to turn a profit, to make money for their shareholders, a factor that certainly plays into their business decisions.

For the purposes of this book, we are going to narrow the definition of "mission-driven work" to organizations that are generally nonprofit or not-for-profit status and who operate in the social sector: healthcare, education, community development, the arts, etc. These organizations are typically funded through philanthropic donations and public or private grants, and they may have a fee-for-service model but are not in the business of turning a profit. It is possible similar stories and experiences stem from for-profit companies, and this book may be helpful for individuals in those situations as well. But the purpose of this book is to highlight the experience of those in the nonprofit sector, because that is where we least expect these stories to happen.

For further clarity, a few examples of local, regional, and national organizations that would fall into this definition are provided in the following table, along with their mission statements taken from each of their websites. These well-known, well-established organizations were selected for illustrative purposes only to help demonstrate the breadth and depth of mission-driven work. To be clear, none of these organizations play any role in the stories told later in this book.

Habitat for Humanity (habitat.org)	Habitat for Humanity's mission is to bring people together to build homes, communities, and hope.
The Southern Poverty Law Center (splcenter.org)	Southern Poverty Law Center is a human rights focused group that works to dismantle White supremacy and confront hate groups. The Southern Poverty Law Center works to protect the most vulnerable groups and individuals in the South and provide resources to those who need them most.

Chicago Public Art Group (chicagopublicartgroup .org)	CPAG unites artists, citizens, and organizations to produce high-quality art reflective of the community where it is placed. The organization mentors, trains, inspires, and supports its artists to create public art throughout Chicago. It educates and teaches creative skills to children and adults, providing them with the tools to articulate their ideas and the confidence to transform their physical environment.
Teach for America (teachforamerica.org)	Teach for America strives to provide quality education for all children in the United States, regardless of their background or socioeconomic status.
Girls Inc. (girlsinc.org)	Girls Inc. partners with schools and utilized organizational centers to assist young girls in developing self-esteem and strength. Through the use of mentoring relationships, pro-girl environments and programs, Girls Inc. works to help girls navigate gender, economic, and social barriers to grow up independently.
Community Hope NJ (communityhope-nj.org)	Our mission is to be a beacon of hope in our community, connecting individuals and families with life-changing support, services, and housing that foster the independence and resiliency to live their best lives.
Visiting Nurses Association (vnahg.org)	Visiting Nurses Association Health Group is a nonprofit organization dedicated to empowering individuals and families to live their best lives, by providing compassionate, coordinated, innovative care in their homes and communities.

These organizations are certainly doing good work. Reading their mission statements leaves one feeling hopeful and optimistic. And again, I am making no claim about the culture at these organizations—they are simply examples of the types of organizations that help define mission-driven work.

Now that we have a common understanding of what is meant by "mission-driven work," we can talk about what makes this work unique.

How Is Mission-Driven Work Different From Any Other Job?

Generally (although not exclusively), people in this work believe deeply in the mission, as seen in the examples at the top of this chapter. At the very least, their personal beliefs and values are aligned with the mission. (Indeed, it would be challenging for an employee of one of these organizations to be completely opposed to the mission and still contribute in good faith to the work of the organization.)

The mission is everywhere, literally. You'll find it on the walls, in the marketing decks, and on the letterhead and website. It is deeply embedded as part of individual employee orientation, goal setting, and the evaluation of progress and success at both the individual and organizational level. There is no escaping it; the mission is at the forefront of the work, just like a figurehead on a ship.

An additional difference is that the bottom line of mission-driven work is measured by the impact it has on humans, not in the amount of dollars made. Of course, there is always a financial component of running a business, even a not-for-profit business. But here, the financial aspects are an input, not an outcome. It's about how the money is used, not whether any is made. The real bottom line is the impact on people. So, when we think about the impact of this work, it has a face—or many faces! They are students, patients, neighbors—people in need.

Why do these two differences—the fact that people generally are committed to the mission and that real humans are on the other side of the work—matter?

Simply stated, they factor into employees' decisions about and their commitment to the work.

On the one hand, it can be incredibly gratifying to know your work and your effort is contributing to something you care about so deeply, and that it matters to people. It can also be rewarding to work with others who have a similar commitment. On the other hand, these differences make it difficult to leave a job, even if that job might not be serving you in the best way. When you leave one of these mission-driven organizations, for any reason at all, it is not uncommon to hear guilt-inducing comments like the following:

> "I'm so sad for the kids who won't get to have you as their teacher!"

> "Oh no! But what about the patients? You've done so much for this program!"

> "Don't you care about this effort anymore?"

These comments might seem inconsequential on the surface, but as someone who has been on the receiving end, I can assure you that they feel anything but. Feelings of guilt and duty (even if it seems irrationally outsized) can become a significant barrier. I have worked with clients to reframe their mindset in an effort to undo the impact of these statements.

Somehow, when working for a cause that means so much to you and to others, the impact of your personal decisions becomes bigger than you. Similar to other jobs, your decisions affect the team of people with whom you work, but they also affect the "bottom line," which, in this case, is also human.

What Does Mission-Driven Work Promise?

The promise of mission-driven work is that your work contributes to a greater good. There is a good feeling associated with working hard to impact people in a positive way. When you take a job at one of these organizations, you know that your work, no matter how far it is from the end product or service, will impact real people.

Take each of the following fictional examples under consideration:

> As an accountant in the finance department at Habitat for Humanity, I know that by supporting the organization to run functionally and continue for years to come, I will be part of providing the infrastructure for the organization to build secure housing for millions of people in need.

> As an artist-in-residence at the Chicago Public Art Group, I am directly enhancing the lives of people in my community.

> As an executive assistant for a leadership team member at Teach for America, I am supporting the organizational functioning that impacts tens of thousands of students every single year.

While doing each of these jobs doesn't necessarily mean you'd come face to face with the people on the other end of the work, you are able to find fulfillment knowing that your work contributes to the functioning of an organization that exists to help people. Your work is one of the pieces necessary for it to function effectively.

Why Does It Matter?

Entering a mission-driven space brings a pervasive sense of optimism. Imagine the onboarding process—it's filled with inspiring stories of impact and pictures of the people who have been influenced positively by the organization thus far. As a result, you develop a strong sense of "I want to help too!"

And frankly, without a strong sense of optimism, mission-driven work in the social sector would not exist. As Noam Chomsky, renowned American professor of linguistics and political activist, so eloquently states, "Optimism is a strategy for making a better future. Because unless you believe that the future can be better, you are unlikely to step up and take responsibility for making it so." Without that sense of optimism, these organizations simply could not exist.

Mission-driven work implies empathy, caring, and heart. We expect to see it every day and to live it in our work lives. We know the work may be challenging, but we also know we are in it with a group of people jointly committed to doing good. What can go wrong?

In this book, we will be joined by five friends who have worked in mission-driven organizations across industries. Their experiences will provide a window into the four-phase cycle that was described at the beginning of this chapter (entering with optimism, a harsh reality, hitting rock bottom, and finding a path forward). You may relate to their stories and feel camaraderie with them as they find a path forward. Or you may learn how to identify these problems in the workplace before they have a chance to impact you or your loved ones.

Before we get too far, however, let's meet the friends who will come along on this journey with us, starting, of course, in their place of promise and optimism.

 Consider heading over to the companion journal for a moment of guided reflection before meeting our friends.

Chapter 2
Meet Our Friends

Now that we have defined what we mean by mission-driven work and learned what makes it unique, it is time to meet the friends who will join us on this journey. Our friends are five women who have each experienced their own unique but all-too-familiar trials in mission-driven nonprofit work. Together, they span roles from entry level to senior-most executive, from people manager to individual contributor. We have young women trying to make their own way in the big city, women who are married with children, and a new mom committed to setting a good example for her daughter. Our friends have graciously shared their stories with us to serve as examples for the learning throughout the book.

Before we begin, please note that these are true stories shared by five brave women. The names of all individuals in the stories as well as any other identifying details, including the names and industries of the organizations in which they were employed, have been fictionalized to protect the privacy of those who have shared. The facts of their stories, however, remain intact.

In this chapter, we will learn about our friends' unique contexts and join them at the optimistic beginning of their journey. We'll start each friend's story with a quote from her interview with me, a snippet that demonstrates her deep connection and personal commitment to the mission of her work.

Without further ado, allow me to introduce our friends: Miah, Briana, Evelyn, Nina, and Faith.

Miah, 49-Year-Old White Female

"I love the actual clinical work... having the privileged opportunity to support people and learn from them... Seeing people travel the path from their most vulnerable state to finding the strength in their recovery; the work is so fundamental to humanity."

Miah was listening to an audiobook as she drove the 75-minute commute to her workplace. She was full of energy and excitement, and the book was a distraction that helped calm her nerves. It was a big day: her first formal presentation to a class of graduate students and a huge step toward formalizing her new role, Manager of Substance Use Disorders and Rehabilitation in the Division of Behavioral Health at Sinclair Hartwell Medical Center in suburban Atlanta.

Miah had worked hard for this career transition. After taking time off to be the primary caregiver for her daughter, she worked in social services at a local nonprofit. After a few years back in the workforce, she followed her passion and became an accredited social worker with a specialty in rehabilitation and recovery. Miah was initially hired at Sinclair Hartwell to work directly with patients in both the in-patient and out-patient programs.

Right away, Miah was passionate about providing support for women and men in recovery, particularly in the community she was serving. Sinclair Hartwell was located in an area which drew on a small population of wealthy White suburban families, but had a larger number of patients who experienced challenging socioeconomic circumstances. Many patients were uninsured or underinsured, people of color, and/or were non-English speakers. She quickly saw the data play out in her day to day.

In the metropolitan Atlanta area, it was widely known that people of color, particularly those living in poverty, were often less likely to receive the mental health services and support required to overcome substance use disorders. As a White woman herself, Miah tried to support her clients as best she could, but she recognized some challenges that came up during moments of vulnerability across lines of difference.

One of the challenges Miah recognized in her first few years was the absence of social workers at Sinclair Hartwell who shared identity markers with the patient community. She also noticed the departments in the Division of Behavioral Health were often at odds—working against one another and competing for resources rather than working together. Miah was somewhat surprised by an undercurrent of judgment that came from the other departments, as if working with addicts was somehow "less no-ble" than working on behalf of neglected children, for example. Miah hoped that moving into a management role would allow her to have an impact on these factors—to build a team that better represented the patient community and build strong re-lationships within and across the division, all while maintaining the high standards of care at the hospital.

Four years into her time at Sinclair Hartwell, the coordinator role became vacant. This role was the senior-most role in her department, and there was no question that Miah wanted to take it on. Despite the fact that stepping into the new role would reduce her patient-facing time, doing so would allow her to ef-fect change in the program and garner a level of respect for their work that had been lacking. She would be in a position to shape the team and make the changes she believed were necessary to better serve the patient population. While the coordinator role did not come with any external validation (no significant salary bump despite the increase in responsibilities) and it didn't bring the level of respect given to the leaders of other departments (which, for some reason, were all led by managers rather than coordinators), it was most certainly a step in the right direction.

While in the coordinator role for just a short time, Miah was able to make significant improvements to the program. Despite the overall low representation of people of color in the social work field, Miah's hiring efforts resulted in a team of 17 with eight people of color, including native and fluent speakers of Spanish to better serve those populations.

Over time, Miah saw a cultural shift start to happen. She bridged the divide between individuals in her department and those who worked in Youth and Family Services. Under her leadership, she saw relationships blossom and respect grow within and between the departments.

Two years into her role as coordinator, the leader of the division resigned and a new director was hired. When the new director, Andie, came on board, she questioned why the Substance Use Disorders and Rehabilitation department was led by a coordinator rather than a manager, and she suggested they work to elevate Miah's role. Andie looked to Miah to take the reins and rewrite the job description, as she had the expertise and the institutional knowledge needed to navigate the tricky waters.

Back in the car on the way to work, Miah was using all of her usual strategies to keep her angst at bay on that important morning. The distraction of the audiobook was helpful, but she also reminded herself that she was prepared. Without being asked, she had done all of the legwork for the proposal, including research on reasonable compensation for the new role. She wanted Andie to be in a strong and well-informed position to approach her superiors, and so far, her efforts had been welcomed.

She would have to worry about her conversation with Andie later, because before going into the office for her normal workday, Miah first needed to stop at the local university to speak to a large group of aspiring professionals. Sometimes she wondered how she managed to set herself up for stressful events like these. But damn, she sure did love her job.

Briana, 33-Year-Old Black Female

"At the beginning, when you see this broad mission, you're thinking, 'I'm aligned with what's happening here; this is great.' And then going through the whole interview process and meeting [a colleague] who I felt was very authentic right away, it felt like the right fit."

Briana took a deep breath as she rode the train to work that Monday. She was three months into her new role as Executive Assistant (EA) to the CEO of the Great Lakes Regional Youth Development Organization (GLY) and had just returned from a long-awaited post-pandemic trip to visit her mother and father. She knew it had been too early to take this much time off, but she hadn't seen her parents in more than two years, and she had notified GLY about this trip before accepting the job. Now back in Wisconsin, Briana was still relishing in the energy of her visit and fresh ties to her homeland and felt eager to get back into the routine.

The central office for GLY was based in Milwaukee and provided the management services for more than 40 chapters across four states: Wisconsin, Illinois, Ohio, and Michigan. A native of Jamaica, Briana had a master's degree in international diplomacy.

Following three successful administrative posts at the Office of International Affairs in Washington, DC, Briana had accepted this role to accompany a move to be closer to her husband's family. The mission of GLY was to provide extracurricular and academic support opportunities for Black and Brown youth in under-resourced communities. Even though this was a new field for Briana, she felt a deep commitment to the mission and to combatting the racial and economic inequities in the country in which she was making her home and raising her child.

So far, the role had been challenging, but she was making good progress. She knew she had the required skills; she just had to learn the unique context of this work and the preferences of her new boss. Because communication and trust were essential in her role as EA, she had spent the first 90 days focused on building relationships—not just with the CEO, but with everyone she came into contact with.

On the train preparing for reentry, Briana thought back over the last three months. Her interview process had unfolded rather quickly. She interviewed with the operations manager first, completed a performance task, and then met the CEO in person to discuss the task. The task was of no concern—she was certain her skill set was a match. And her conversation with the operations manager was fantastic. Briana felt a clear connection there and was happy to know she would be working closely with her. When she met Linda, the CEO, she sensed a small flutter of doubt deep in her belly… but couldn't put her finger on why it was there. Briana reasoned it was nerves, both hers and Linda's.

On her first day, she was eager to get to know her new colleagues and build upon the relationship with the operations manager that had started during the interview process. When Briana arrived that day, though, she was directed to her desk located right next to Linda's office. That seemed logical, but what didn't make sense was that it was separated physically from the rest of the in-office staff. Between the physical separation and recalling the weird feeling at the interview, Briana felt that flutter begin to surface again. But soon enough, she was too busy to give it another thought.

It wasn't long before Briana recognized that Linda was going to be a demanding boss. She had a high bar of excellence that left little room for error. But Briana had always been a hard worker and held herself to high standards, so that didn't worry her much. Besides, their work was important—it was important to do excellent work on behalf of the children they served.

And Linda was clearly excited about hiring Briana. She greeted her with enthusiasm each morning, spent time providing context for things she was working on, and generally seemed invested in helping Briana learn about their work. Linda had a mantra that kept the importance of the mission in the forefront of everyone's mind: "Behave each day as if the youth are watching." Briana loved this idea to keep her grounded in impact.

After long days in the office, Briana was tired every night and was perhaps a little put off that the 9 o'clock start time had effectively become "8:30 or you're late," but she chalked it all up to being relatively new to her role. With a four-year-old daughter at home, it was hard to feel so tired and still find the energy to show up as a good mom, but she was making it work.

She was committed to being the trusted confidante any CEO would love to have and was sure that everything would even out as time went on. In the first three months, there were no major mishaps and Briana assessed she was on the right track in terms of building a strong relationship with Linda.

As hard as it was to go back to work after a vacation, Briana discovered she was excited about the impact of GLY as an organization and was eager to move into the next phase of the role.

Evelyn, 28-Year-Old White Female

"I was really impressed by their work. Think about it—we fly rich men around the world to learn at conferences, but we don't fly poor women around—and who needs it more? This organization sponsored scholarships to attend international educational initiatives for poor women from developing countries, allowing them access to knowledge typically reserved for the privileged. Having come out of two years of learning about the international system, it was kind of revolutionary, because these women were disrupting the system!"

As Evelyn moved her final boxes into the tiny apartment she would be sharing with two graduate school friends, she thought about how lucky she was. She had just graduated with her master's degree in international relations and her internship had turned into a full-time job offer. Actually, it was a part-time job, but it was all the organization could afford at the time, and she eagerly accepted, having been worried about the crumbling US economy. It was 2008, after all.

A native of Brussels, Evelyn had completed both her undergraduate and graduate degrees in Belgium, at a university that had a great relationship with US-based NGOs. During her final year of her master's program, she had been connected with the Rise Foundation, a highly respected international women's rights organization based in San Francisco.

For the fall semester, Evelyn paid full tuition at her university to work with a group of classmates on a research project for the organization, the output of which was then delivered to the company, free of charge. When the project was completed, the team was able to visit the Rise office in person.

On her first visit to the San Francisco office, Evelyn remembers being awed from the moment she saw the building. The office was a piece of history in and of itself—it was a classic Victorian row house with a plaque commemorating the building as a historic landmark. And the women who ran the organization—talk about impressive! The current executive director and many of the current board members had been front and center during the women's rights movement in the late '60s and early '70s, participating in demonstrations and fighting for the passage of the Equal Rights Amendment, Title IX, and *Roe vs. Wade*. I mean, what young feminist wouldn't want to contribute to the mission of these visionaries who had done so much for the movement more than 30 years ago?

Evelyn settled into her apartment and talked herself through it again. She had crunched the numbers—her measly salary would pay for her share of the rent and her food, *if* she was careful about spending! Since it was part time for now, she would have time to pick up a waitressing job or—god forbid—a babysitting gig. *Really? Is this what earning a master's degree gets me?* she thought. Rise didn't offer health insurance since all employees were classified as consultants, but she was pretty healthy so—fingers crossed! All things considered, Evelyn figured it had to be a net positive. She was doing work that made a difference, her organization was supporting her work visa, and she was grateful to have more opportunities than the women her organization served, that's for sure.

Rise had been an outgrowth of local feminist activism into something powerful with a more global reach. They were looking at transforming systems of aid given just how flawed the United Nations system had become. They believed voices of women were not being taken into account, not only in America but also globally. As a result, the whole mission of Rise was to fund, uplift, empower, and give voice to community-based efforts led by women in developing countries all over the world.

So, yes, Evelyn could see her privilege when taking that context into account.

Evelyn would start her work as a part-time consultant, no longer a student intern. She looked forward to working alongside these feminist icons, contributing more to the mission than she had been able to as a student, and helping to build a positive culture for the employees like her who were struggling to make ends meet, all while making a difference for women in need.

Nina, 32-Year-Old Latina

> "When I thought about the mission of the organization and the work they were doing, I always thought of that girl who sat next to me in keyboarding, whose name I never knew. But she knew very well that I had a certain privilege she didn't… Of course I want to work at an organization like this, you know?"

On a Friday afternoon in the fall of 2022, Nina checked her email one last time before the weekend and saw her acceptance to the 2023 cohort of the American Equity Corps (AEC). She was thrilled! What an opportunity to meet equity leaders from other organizations and to contribute to the tremendous learning culture of her work family at the Partnership for the Arts (PArts).

Nina had joined PArts as a marketing associate in late 2020 and had settled nicely into her role at the organization. Even though she had no background in the arts, she was excited by the mission and felt personally connected to it. The mission of PArts, a nonprofit organization based in Austin, Texas, with national reach, was to improve access to arts programming both in and out of school for students living in underserved communities. Nina remembers connecting the mission to her own experience with privilege while preparing for her interview. As a Latina who had grown up in a predominantly White suburb, Nina was always aware of race and the implications it had on opportunities. She understood privilege as well.

Nina still recalls sitting in her keyboarding class in the late '90s and completing her typing assignments on the class set of word processors. The girl who sat next to her was one of the only Black students in the school. Her family had petitioned for her to attend that school instead of the failing school in her home district. During class one day, this student turned to Nina and asked, "You have a computer at home, don't you?" At that moment, Nina felt her privilege hit her over the head. She hadn't recognized the advantage that having a computer at home would have on her opportunity to succeed in this class, and this one comment had made it so clear.

So, when Nina was considering the job at PArts, she thought of the girl in keyboarding class. She wanted to use her skills to support the organization that was fighting to bring opportunity and access to students who otherwise would not have it. And more importantly, she brought strong skills in marketing and digital media to her role—a much needed fill of the gap in skill among the current staff!

Nina's first few years at PArts were challenging and inspiring. As a relatively small organization, her role evolved over time. Yes, she was primarily responsible for marketing tasks, but what did that look like at PArts? Most of her big projects were related to website development and advertising since PArts didn't have traditional marketing needs. Her projects included a few event launches and social media campaigns for arts advocacy. She quickly learned that supporting the team's all-hands meetings was also part of her core responsibilities. As a remote-first workplace, the team came together three times a year for a multi-day gathering which they referred to as the all-hands meeting. Nina wasn't sure why, but she was tasked with planning and organizing many of those meetings.

And wow—the all-hands gatherings were inspiring! Composed of a group of incredibly talented former arts educators, the team at PArts was committed to being lifelong learners. It didn't matter that Nina came without experience in the field, she—and the team around her—engaged in deep learning every time they were gathered together.

Nina was challenged on a daily basis, and her contributions to the work grew. She had joined the organization during a time of turbulence and transition, as the country was getting used to life following a global pandemic. The response from leadership was humane, showing flexibility and kindness both to employees and grant recipients. It was a learning experience for Nina just to observe the leadership needed to make a smooth transition in the context of what was going on in the world.

In 2021, along with many organizations across the nation, PArts was confronted with a deep racial reckoning. As an organization designed to serve the underserved by disrupting the barriers of racism and poverty, were they doing all they could? They were an organization composed primarily of White women. What were they really doing for Black and Brown children? And could they do better?

As a result of this equity work, PArts implemented a complete overhaul to their organizational structure to increase representation in the decision-making process. In addition, PArts decided to sponsor two employees to apply for the American Equity Corps. Nina was thrilled to be a part of it, but the way she was asked had left a bad taste in her mouth. The person who invited her to apply had explained the AEC and said that her colleague, Jade, would be Nina's partner on the application. "We were going to send a White woman with Jade, but thought it might be good for PArts to be represented by a non-Black person of color." Nina wished the invitation had been delivered with a different tone. Perhaps something like, "We think you'll represent us well." Or, "You have the skills to turnkey your learning to the organization." Instead she got, "You are our second choice, and we're picking you because you are Latina."

While it wasn't the greatest rationale, Nina was still thrilled for the opportunity. She was committed to representing the organization well and to learning all she could about equity in the workplace and the world. Not only was the work of PArts important, so was the work of anti-racism and equity. And besides, the person who was responsible for the offending invitation wasn't her boss, wasn't the senior-most leader of the organization, and didn't hold any obvious power over her, so Nina let it slide. She couldn't wait to get started with the AEC!

Faith, 39-Year-Old Black Female

"I knew this district, from the administration to the teachers and the students. This district had my heart. I had given so much of myself to this work, and I longed to be the one to lead us into our next phase of success. I knew I had the skills, and I knew I could do it with the right team surrounding me. I could not have been more excited to lean into this work."

Faith hit send on the email announcing her two new hires. If she was going to make it as this district's senior-most executive, she couldn't do it without a strong deputy and a supportive, detail-oriented executive assistant.

Seventeen years prior, Faith took her first teaching job after graduating from UNC Chapel Hill. She was hired at a middle school in Atlanta and jumped in with two feet, eager to make a difference in the lives of her students. Unfortunately, she learned a hard lesson that first year: a bad leader can make your life a living hell. For some reason, the principal of her school had it out for Faith. To this day, she doesn't know what was behind it, but that first year was terrible. The other new teachers hadn't experienced the same hostility, and the more tenured teachers saw what was happening and took Faith under their collective wing. "I don't know why she's doing this to you, but come sit with us, and we'll protect you," was their message.

Toward the end of the year, during a building visit, a district administrator witnessed an interaction between Faith and her principal, one that, to Faith, had become a common occurrence. The principal had popped her head into Faith's classroom and berated her for the noise level coming from her room. Faith's students had been actively engaged in a learning activity, and the energy and volume were evidence of their collective enthusiasm. A little noisy, but not unreasonable.

Later, when her students had left for the day, the visiting administrator returned to her classroom and sat down. He said, "Don't you ever let anybody treat you like that again. I watched it. I saw you shaking. I saw her finding joy in causing this reaction. Please don't quit, but please don't let her win." He must have spoken to the principal about it as well, because she apologized for that interaction (as if it were an anomaly) and backed off for a while. But at the start of the second year, their relationship was back to business as usual.

At the end of December break her second year, Faith came down with pneumonia while visiting her family in Virginia. After calling out sick to give herself time to recover, she ended up taking a medical leave of absence. A follow-up with her primary care physician revealed some concerning facts: Faith was losing weight at a rapid rate, most likely due to stress.

This did not go over well with the principal, and after seemingly endless rounds of back and forth about whether or not her leave was medically necessary, Faith decided to put her health first and break her contract with the district. She was devastated for her students but knew she had to prioritize her physical and mental health. Faith moved back home to Virginia and started temping.

So how on Earth did she end up taking on the role of Interim Superintendent of the Richfield Public School District? What a journey it had been.

Shortly after returning to Virginia and her hometown of Richfield, Faith was approached by a recruiter about taking on a history teacher position in one of the local middle schools. Knowing her strong work ethic and experience, many people had referred her for the role. She initially said no. After all, she was still recovering from the tough situation in Atlanta and wasn't ready to give it another shot. But the recruiter was unrelenting. She invited Faith to interview and visit the school, and Faith was hired on the spot.

Faith's career began advancing and expanding before she even got settled in the school. She was quickly recognized as one of the strongest teachers in the school and was asked to provide coaching and demo lessons to other teachers. After making a difference in the school's instructional practices, Faith was asked to tackle school culture, which was in dire need of improvement.

Next she was tapped by the superintendent, Erin Hayes, first to take over as principal of a turnaround school—one that was going to have to close its doors if it didn't improve—and then to be the founding principal of their expansion middle school. Faith continued to thrive in each and every role.

In thinking about her success in these roles, Faith always recalls her formative experience with that principal in Atlanta. She knew what it had felt like to be dehumanized and devalued in her work, and she vowed to never do that to anyone who worked for or with her. Even when she had to terminate an employee or take disciplinary action, she did so with grace and kindness. It was truly an honor to be able to lead with compassion, make a difference for teachers and students, and ensure that she was not repeating the cycle of abuse she herself had endured.

Just when Faith thought she was settled into a long-term role after nine years of hopping around in the district, Superintendent Hayes approached her once again, this time about applying for the role of assistant superintendent of operations. This was a huge job. It involved managing a team at the central office with responsibility for transportation, buildings and grounds, and emergency preparedness, among other things.

Most of all, the role involved being both the public face and the operational leader for any and all crises that the district might face. Erin Hayes had seen the leadership potential in Faith all along, and she was opening the door to an amazing opportunity for her.

While she was sad to leave her school community behind, Faith decided to apply and was offered the job without reservation.

The role was not without challenge. Faith was a relatively young Black woman who was now seated at the executive leadership table with mostly older White men. While Erin, as superintendent, was clearly on her side, Faith had to jump through a lot of hoops to get her peers to listen to her, respect her, and see her as a true part of the team. As soon as she was hired, one of her direct reports refused to report to her and demanded that he be moved to reporting directly to Superintendent Hayes.

Despite this uphill battle, Faith saw immediate success. She rebuilt the team, got them working together, and managed a major crisis. Faith felt like she was in just the right role to suit her strengths. Levelheaded and an extroverted go-getter, this role was perfect for Faith.

Five years later, RPSD experienced a period of turnover. Erin Hayes had followed her lifelong dream to resign her position in the district and start a business, and a new superintendent had been hired. Shortly after, Faith took parental leave with her first child. She returned to her operations job anticipating the challenge as a new mom of an infant. Just a few weeks after Faith returned, the new superintendent shocked the board by resigning only three months into his tenure.

Having heard so much from Erin for years about Faith's ability to put out any fire, to come into tough situations and "handle them," the board approached Faith about taking on the interim superintendency. Faith knew how much it was going to take to right this ship that had lost a longtime leader and had just suffered another blow with the sudden departure of the new superintendent.

At the same time, Faith had a track record of success in taking on challenges in this district and had successfully led several change management efforts at scale. Beyond that, Faith cared so deeply about the students and the teachers in the district. Now that she was a mom, her passion was profoundly personal. She would do everything she could to be sure the district was good enough for her own daughter.

Faith reached out to Erin for advice as her long-term mentor and friend, and Erin reiterated that she had left the district in a good place and there wouldn't be any hidden surprises. Erin believed in Faith and knew in her heart that she was well poised to be the next leader of RPSD. Faith accepted the board's terms without negotiation, rolled up her sleeves, and got to work. Her first order of business was getting her two core team members hired, and then, together, they would tackle what needed to be done.

Now two months into the role, Faith had found her people. She was filled with cautious optimism and a deep commitment to the entire school community as she hit send on the introductory email.

 Consider taking a moment in the companion journal to process what you've learned about each of our friends.

PART II

Discovering a Harsh Reality

"The culture of a workplace—an organization's values, norms, and practices— has a huge impact on our happiness and success."

— Adam Grant

Chapter 3
Toxic Work Culture Defined

In Chapter 2, we met our friends and learned a little bit about their background and how they came into the roles they have now. We felt their optimism and the depth of their personal connection with the work. At the end of each story thus far, we are left standing with them on the precipice of what we now know will be the discovery of a harsh reality. In some cases, we have seen warning signs, but in all cases, our friends are still holding on to hope.

Before we go down the path of discovery with our friends, let's take a moment to step out of their stories and discuss the idea of toxic work culture. We will look at some of the behaviors that result in a problematic environment and why "toxic" is such an appropriate word to describe this culture. In addition to looking at specific observable behaviors and experiences, we will analyze the different ways toxic culture can be present in working environments, from personnel management, organizational leadership, and team dynamics to generally accepted behavioral norms organization-wide.

Importantly, in this chapter we will go one step further and connect toxic work culture with mission-driven work. While we often hear about these experiences happening in corporate, for-profit environments, our friends are here to show that toxic culture can be prevalent in mission-driven work as well. We will discuss the unique impact culture has in a mission-driven environment because of the kinds of people who are drawn to this work and the commitment to the mission.

Toxic Work Culture

Anyone active in business-related discussions on social media these days knows that "toxic work culture" is a hot topic being discussed day in and day out. I see it every day. Posts with headlines like "10 indications you have a toxic boss" and "how do you know if your workplace is toxic" litter the feeds of users with a professional slant to their algorithm. Employees, managers, executives, and board members can all be "toxic," as can meetings, one-on-one relationships, situations, and teams. But what exactly is "toxic work culture" and why does the word "toxic" fit so well?

The term "toxic work environment" was first used in the metaphorical sense that it is used today in a 1989 publication in the field of nursing. While the term had previously been used literally when describing work environments filled with chemicals and other pollutants, the American Historical Association identifies this as the first use of the term with today's meaning.

The *Guide to Leadership in Nursing* described toxic work environments as those that included "poorly articulated goals, a winner-take-all approach to conflicts, and a 'one right way' attitude toward completing tasks," and in the nursing field in particular, a toxic environment featured "top-down decision making, low morale, sexual harassment, unequal pay, and job insecurity." [1]

Today, the definition of toxic work culture remains fairly consistent. According to Wikipedia:

> A "toxic workplace" is a colloquial metaphor used to describe a place of work, usually an office environment, that is marked by significant personal conflicts between those who work there. Toxic workplaces are created by the actions of toxic employers and/or employees; that is, individuals who are motivated by personal gain, whether driven by power, money, fame, or special status, utilize unethical means or behaviors to psychologically manipulate, belittle, or frustrate those around them, or divert attention away from their personal inadequate performance or misdeeds. [2]

We will spend more time in this book looking at specific instances of toxicity at work, but first, let's talk about why toxic is a term that seems so fitting.

Another word for toxic is poisonous. Something that is poisonous spreads and threatens the health of the individual and the environment in which it is trying to thrive. Toxic leaders, toxic behaviors, toxic teams, toxic relationships... Experiencing any or all of these is like being exposed to a poison that threatens the health of the person who is trying to thrive in an organization. On a larger scale, these poisons threaten the health and vitality of the organization itself.

While it feels harsh to describe human behavior as poisonous, this lens helps us to frame the effort it takes for an individual to overcome its effects. The metaphor simply works. So let's talk about the poison itself, and then we will address how it spreads.

What's the Poison?

Healthy organizations require, at a minimum, a certain level of professionalism and an environment built on trust and psychological safety. Toxic work culture can emerge from the absence of these minimums and can show up in a variety of observable behaviors. What's hard is that situations involving these behaviors are easy to overlook as isolated incidents—anyone can have a bad day, right? But left unaddressed, these behaviors can take over like a poison infecting a single body or an entire community.

Just as there are many poisonous elements in the natural world, workplace toxicity exists in many forms as well. In this book, we'll cover a few of the more common types found in mission-driven organizations. On one end of the spectrum are behaviors that contribute to a lack of professional standards or boundaries or lack of trust and safety. On the other end is narcissistic abuse and abuse of power. Many of these behaviors overlap, and while there are certainly others to consider, this will give us a place to start the discussion.

Lack of Professionalism

Toxic culture can often emerge from a casual, informal environment, one that typically overdials on the "family" or "we're all friends here, we don't need all those rules and expectations" narrative. This phenomena is common in smaller organizations, ones that start off with a familial feeling, or those started by people who are actually related. Many mission-driven organizations are born from passion projects among friends and family, so it's easy to maintain and carry forward a fairly casual environment.

But when the organization grows and more people are brought on to the team, care needs to be taken to ensure that professional standards are established. This might be as simple as respecting boundaries of employees, drawing a line between the personal and professional.

While it seems innocuous at first, left unchecked, it's easy to get into a sticky situation in which employees are being treated unprofessionally.

Consider a family-run foundation hiring its first non-relative employee. Perhaps the coffee-break and water-cooler conversations have, to date, regularly skirted into topics such as relationships, children, and personal finances. While that might be tolerated in a family setting, it would be completely inappropriate for the new hire. In such circumstances, it is often hard for the employee to speak up about the behavior, because the employee will be seen as speaking out "against the family" and small organizations don't provide much opportunity for anonymity.

Another way that lack of professionalism shows up, particularly in nonprofit organizations, is through meager compensation and lack of benefits. Low compensation is often justified by the claim that "the privilege to do this work is compensation in and of itself." [3] Low pay and lack of good health benefits puts additional stress on workers and causes them to feel, at best, undervalued, and, at worst, dehumanized.

As a person who has worked in K-12 education, the number of times I have heard, "Well, you didn't get into teaching for the money, right?" is alarming. It's a glorification of low pay that is simply unprofessional.

In our friends' stories in the next chapters, we will see examples of low pay, lack of benefits, and professional boundary crossing—taking the casual workplace to an extreme that makes employees feel uncomfortable and unsafe.

Nonexistent Boundaries

We've already touched on boundaries with respect to professional interactions. Another place where lack of boundaries can cause toxic culture is related to time. This applies in situations in which around-the-clock work is expected, or when staying late at the office and "pitching in" well above and beyond the job's requirements is celebrated and encouraged.

This expectation can lead to organizations where overwork is a systemic issue. All too often, the onus to carve out and protect space for our nonwork selves falls on workers. Common anti-burnout advice such as "set boundaries" and "practice self-care" crumbles without institutional support. If your company is chronically understaffed or your pay is tied to your hours, the right choice is often a difficult, or even impossible, choice to make. [4]

In our friends' stories, we will see examples of managers requiring employees to be on call "at all times," expecting attendance at work functions when they are unwell and full-time access while being compensated for part-time work.

Inequity and Lack of Humanity in Treatment of Employees

One of the most common causes of a toxic workplace is the unexplained and indefensible inequitable treatment of employees across an organization. This does not mean that everyone must be held to exactly the same expectations all the time. Equity is not synonymous with lack of flexibility.

A common reflection of people who have experienced a toxic work environment is that they felt dehumanized or unseen. This can happen when people aren't recognized for the full human experience they are having (for example, when an employee is struggling with a terminal family illness and compassion and flexibility are not granted). Employees are humans with complex lives full of challenges and experiences outside of the workplace.

A healthy work culture respects those aspects of their employees' lives. They honor their experience and acknowledge the effect that outside challenges may have on their ability to do their job. This has to be done, of course, while keeping the work in mind, but often these tensions can be addressed in a way that honors both the people and the work.

At the same time, there must be some consistency in the way employees are treated. One person can't be given complete flexibility and support through a challenging situation while another is denied that compassion. When people are treated differently within the same organization and can't see a defensible reason as to why that might be the case, it breeds distrust.

In our friends' stories, we will see examples of every iteration of this—flexibility not being granted, compassion not being shown, using "consistency" as the excuse for rigidity, and people with similar circumstances being treated in different ways.

Lack of Trust and Safety

Well-known management consultant Patrick Lencioni has written bestselling books about the components of a functional team and what it takes for organizations to succeed. In his two books, *The Five Dysfunctions of a Team* and *The Advantage*, Lencioni identifies five critical behaviors for strong teams.

The following diagram shows the relationship of those five behaviors:

As the image shows, **trust** is the foundation of a strong and
functional team. A team that does not have trust will not achieve
their highest potential, let alone accomplish much of the work
it sets out to do. Trust in the workplace is often thought of as "I
can count on you to do what you say you are going to do." That
dependability certainly is a part of it, but Lencioni goes further
to say that trust on a team needs to be *vulnerability-based trust.*
A strong team is created in an environment in which every member feels comfortable being vulnerable, admitting what they
don't know, coming clean when they have made mistakes, and

accepting responsibility for their actions. [5] In my experience, some of the toughest teams I have worked on or with have lacked this foundational element of trust. Even when they finally recognized its absence, it was nearly impossible to rebuild.

Another element of strong teams is a shared commitment to common goals. Team members with a self-serving orientation do nothing to further the shared commitments. Toxic work culture develops when there is an "every man for himself" approach to problem solving. Behaviors indicative of this kind of environment can be subtle: quietly undermining decisions of leaders or peers to one's "closest friends," or even passive resistance to a collective commitment.

Passive resistance occurs when a decision is made and a leader chooses not to bring the decision to his team. They don't actively work against it, but they also don't actively cascade the decision to their direct reports. This can be incredibly dangerous to organizational culture, as it pits leaders and teams against one another and puts the dysfunction of the leadership team on full display. [6]

Psychological safety shows up as a team's shared belief that each member is truly valued and safe to share ideas, express concerns and admit mistakes, all without fear of negative consequences. Psychological safety has a significantly higher impact on organizational health, team culture, and employee engagement than any other single factor. Behaviors that impact psychological safety include ratio of talk time in meetings, response to "bad news," how (and whether) feedback is solicited or given, and how decisions are made.

For example, when psychological safety does not exist on a team, any or all of the following behaviors can be observed:

- Discussions about problems and mistakes are focused on blame and "how could this happen" as opposed to solutions.

- Mistakes are repeatedly brought up, even when they have been resolved and lessons have been learned.

- Meetings are dominated by one voice or a vocal minority.

- Questions and concerns are dismissed or rationalized.

- Feedback is avoided.

- Decisions are made in a way that is unclear to those who are impacted by the decision.

All of these behaviors contribute to a toxic work environment and cause employees to disengage and question their value.

In our friends' stories, we will see this play out across many different scenarios. Our friends will be ignored when concerns are raised, and they will have peers and managers who undermine their work and their goals, who deny responsibility for their own actions, and who prioritize their own needs over the needs of the team as a whole.

Abuse of Power / Narcissistic Abuse

Within every organization exists a **power dynamic**, whether implicit or explicit. If there is a hierarchy, an inherent power dynamic is associated with it. Additionally, specific attributes that individual employees carry can contribute to hidden power differentials as well: age, longevity, gender, race, or even interpersonal relationships with people who are in other positions of power.

When power dynamics are not called out and addressed, it is easy for them to be abused and for those who are not in positions of power to suffer from that dynamic. Consider a team with a newly hired member who doesn't feel as if their voice is valued in the discussion. Or a peer who has been at the organization a long time and dismisses concerns or new ideas with "that's just how it's done here."

As we climb up the ladder of toxicity, from general lack of professionalism, lack of trust, and psychological safety to taking advantage of positions of power, we reach one of the more extreme forms of a toxic work environment: a narcissistic leader.

Narcissistic abuse is trauma that is experienced when someone is in a relationship with a person who exhibits narcissistic patterns of behavior. Narcissistic personality disorder is not uncommon among high ranking leaders, including those in mission-driven work, as the people in those positions are often charismatic, passionate, well spoken, and have a "shiny" exterior that protects their bad behavior. [7] The narcissistic behavior patterns are often only demonstrated behind closed doors, making them invisible to the general public. Thus, the public impression of the individual is positive, dynamic, and often inspirational, while only the victim sees beyond the shiny exterior. The cost is the dignity, humanity, and often the health of the abused.

A formal diagnosis of narcissistic personality disorder according to the *Diagnostic and Statistical Manual of Mental Disorders*, Fifth Edition, requires that the person exhibit at least five of nine identified behavioral criteria. But we are not here to formally diagnose our coworkers—this work is most certainly best left to the professionals. And frankly, the diagnosis isn't relevant for our discussion. What matters is that the person suffering the abuse is able to identify the abusive behavior, name it, and find a way to heal from it. In her book, *It's Not You: Identifying and Healing from Narcissistic People*, Dr. Ramani Durvasula says this beautifully:

> Identifying a narcissistic person is far less important than understanding what qualifies as unacceptable behavior and what it does to you. In my years of experience working with survivors, I have seen that most people improve significantly when they finally receive validation about the toxicity of the behavior in their relationship, at which point we can start to nudge away the self-blame and begin to heal. [8]

So what does narcissistic abuse look like in the workplace? Of the many patterns of behavior that are evident in a relationship with a narcissist, two are particularly prevalent in a toxic workplace: gaslighting and the DIMMER patterns (a term developed by Dr. Durvasula to refer to dismissiveness, invalidation, minimization, manipulation, exploitativeness, and rage). [9] What makes these patterns of behavior especially hard to deal with is that the narcissist doesn't see the patterns and won't see them when they are pointed out.

Gaslighting is one of the most commonly noted behaviors of toxic leaders. Gaslighting involves the denial of your perspective, which could involve refuting actual events, behaviors, words, actions, or even experiences that you had. When you are being gaslighted by a manager, you will start to feel an urge to overcompensate with evidence: saving emails, texts, and writing down notes from conversations. Your energy goes into building an evidence base for when the person denies your reality instead of into productive two-way communication. The impact of gaslighting is self-doubt. One often starts to think, *Am I crazy?* when someone is constantly telling you that your perspective is wrong.

And it's easy to see why confronting a gaslighter with their behavior is so futile! They'll just deny that too.

The **DIMMER patterns** of behavior, when exhibited by a leader, result in employees feeling small and worthless. Their needs, feelings, beliefs, experiences, thoughts, hopes, and even sense of self are dismissed and invalidated. [10] An example of each type of behavior in the workplace is provided in the following list; consider how the individual's sense of self-worth is impacted by these repetitive interactions.

- **Dismissiveness**: An employee brings a concern to her manager, and the manager's response is to brush it off.

- **Invalidation**: An employee asks for flexibility to address a medical issue and requests are repeatedly ignored or denied; eventually the employee stops asking, getting the message that her health is not a priority.

- **Minimization**: An employee's experiences or accomplishments are minimized in front of the team. "She is new to *this* industry, so all of that doesn't matter much." At the same time, the manager shares her own out-of-industry experience as highly valuable.

- **Manipulation**: A manager leans into vulnerable emotions (like guilt and obligation) to get you to do what they want rather than just asking. "Oh, I just don't know how I am going to finish this task by Monday. We did so much for you when you were out sick last week, I am so far behind."

- **Exploitativeness**: A manager's manipulation may go so far as to be exploitative when they constantly remind an employee of the one favor they did for them sometime in the past to get the person to do work that is above and beyond reasonable expectations.

- **Rage**: A manager reacts to bad news by yelling at her employee in an open office space, telling the employee that her mistakes are what led to this outcome. Later, the manager may shower the employee with compliments or (as noted above) deny having lost her cool in front of others in the office.

These behaviors, especially when experienced day in and day out and in unpredictable ways, can take a tremendous toll on the mental and even physical health of the individuals who experience them and the organizational culture as a whole.

In our friends' stories, we will see managers who display narcissistic patterns. These managers will undermine our friends, act in ways that destabilize them and break their confidence, and rewrite history in ways that make our friends question their own perspective. We will also see peers with unstated relational power take advantage of that power to dominate and diminish our friends.

Where and How Does the Poison Spread?

A poison needs a body or other environment in which to spread, and in the workplace, the body is generally in the form of interpersonal relationships. Any interpersonal relationship or set of relationships can be the origin of a toxic work culture. Toxic culture can sprout in manager–employee relationships, peer-to-peer interactions, team dynamics, and, eventually, overall company culture. An organization which tolerates toxic behavior between individual employees becomes a toxic organization as a whole as such behaviors are witnessed and begin to spread.

The manager–employee relationship is one of the most important relationships in the workplace. In my experience, I have had more than 10 different managers, and I was unequivocally happiest and most productive when I was working for a manager with whom I had a good relationship—a manager who I respected, who respected me, who pushed me and challenged me, but also allowed me to make, and learn from, mistakes.

One of the most difficult relationships in which to endure abuse is the relationship with one's boss. The person to whom you report is quite often responsible for a large part of your daily work experience. They can set the tone for your day to day, they manage your workload, and they are responsible for your job security—in most cases, they can terminate your employment at any time.

In short, they have the power to make your life miserable.

Due to the relative position of power, the manager is in a prime spot for abusive behavior, should that person have any narcissistic tendencies.

That said, power comes in many forms, and abusive relationships are not limited to manager–employee relationships. It is possible to experience narcissistic abuse and general abuse of power with peers as well. Power is not always explicit; it can be informal and implicit as well. Power can also be self-assigned, which inherently results in the opportunity for toxic relationships at any level of organizational structure.

Toxic behavior in any of these one-on-one relationships can spread to teams and then to full organizations. People on teams witness the abusive behavior and see it go unaddressed, and then trust in the team or the organization more broadly begins to crumble. As this poison spreads, it can take over the entire organization, even if employees try to resist. Once the overall company culture is toxic, it is difficult (although not impossible) to reverse.

Not at My Organization!

We've all heard the stories about toxic workplaces on Wall Street, in corporate culture, in places where the bottom line is making money for shareholders or investors. In her book, *Bully Market: My Story of Money and Misogyny at Goldman Sachs,* Jamie Fiore Higgins portrays one such environment. Higgins was an up-and-coming managing director at Goldman Sachs, something only a small percentage of women achieve. By all accounts, she was a raging success. Except that she was miserable and worried about where she was headed.

As her memoir tells, the toxic culture she endured to get where she was in the company was enough to break anyone down. Higgins faced sexist comments on a regular basis. She was silenced when she tried to report unethical behavior. Her choices as a woman were controlled by her male supervisors. For example, despite having access to extensive lactation support services and benefits that the company "valued," on her first day back following her maternity leave, her boss said in no uncertain terms that she would be wise not to continue breastfeeding, as that was time she should be spending at her desk. Veiled (and sometimes not-so-veiled) threats of what would happen to her career if she dismissed the advice were rampant. [11]

But let's go back to our mission-driven spaces, where money is not the bottom line, where people are there to do work that changes the world. These are well-meaning, well-intentioned workplaces that are working to improve humanity, not to increase the profit margins for stakeholders. Is it possible this culture could be prevalent there as well?

Of course! Because even mission-driven organizations are run by humans, and humans bring their full, faulty selves to work! And when those faults show up and are not called out and rectified, they continue to grow and take over the workplace until the toxic culture is pervasive. The impact of this is even more jarring for the mission-driven organization that explicitly states their values—which are in direct conflict with the toxic behaviors.

Learning From Our Friends' Experiences

As organizational psychologist and bestselling author Adam Grant reminds us, "The culture of a workplace—an organization's values, norms and practices—has a huge impact on our happiness and success." The behaviors, norms, and values that are tolerated at an organization impact our success and happiness as employees. We are soon going to have a front row seat to watch this play out in our friends' stories.

In Part I, we met our friends and saw how each was passionate about their work and cautiously optimistic about their respective situations. Despite a few yellow or red flags, all our friends were committed to the work they were doing, were excited about the potential it held, and were on the verge of doing something great.

Spoiler alert: That's all about to change. In the book *Good Enough Job,* Simone Stolzhoff shares the story of Divya, a successful entrepreneur who had a strong relationship with her mentor and cofounder. After a few years of working around the clock, Divya burned out and decided to leave the company. The relationship with her mentor turned sour and he cut her out of ownership of the company without discussion. Divya said, "It was like family, until it wasn't." [12]

In their interviews, each of our friends shared a version of this statement to represent the shock of reality they experienced:

"I loved my job, until I didn't."

"Everyone had my back, until they didn't."

"As an organization, we showed care and compassion for our colleagues, until I was the one who needed it."

In the next five chapters, we will return to our friends' stories to witness how toxic culture can emerge in mission-driven work. We will see how the elements discussed in this chapter—narcissistic abuse, abuse of power, lack of professionalism, and lack of trust and safety—can show up in many ways in mission-driven spaces. As we read the stories of our friends, we will start to be able to give a label to their experiences and identify where the toxicity lies.

As you read the stories of our friends, some aspects might sound familiar. You might recognize portions of their experience in your own workplace, or they might remind you of conversations you've had with a friend or a family member about their work experience. If that's you, fear not; you are not alone. Keep reading.

 Before diving back into our friends' stories, head over to the companion journal to reflect on what you've learned about toxic work culture.

Chapter 4

Miah's Efforts Are Thwarted

In this chapter, we pick up Miah's story where we left off in Chapter 2. Recall that Miah has been working at Sinclair Hartwell Medical Center for a few years and is currently in the role of coordinator of the Substance Use Disorders and Rehabilitation (SUDR) department. In collaboration with the new director, she is working to elevate the role to manager to build upon the growth that occurred under her leadership as coordinator. Miah is anxious about solidifying her promotion and is dealing with the additional stress of speaking to graduate students for the first time.

As you learn more about Miah's experience, tune into which aspects of toxic work culture you notice. At the end of this chapter, we will take a step back and discuss some of the toxic behaviors we see.

Destabilized

As Miah pulled into the parking lot for her presentation, her phone dinged with an incoming text. She saw that it was Andie, so she picked up quickly, thinking it was going to be a quick "go get 'em" pep talk for her presentation.

> Miah, I received your document. You shouldn't assume you would have anything to do with this conversation.

Immediately, Miah felt like she had been kicked in the gut. Oh god, she had overstepped. She had thought she was being proactive. Where had she gone wrong? Andie herself had advocated for the change from coordinator to manager. Miah had developed the job description, even putting it into Andie's preferred format, wanting to take the burden off of Andie as she got her bearings in her new role. Miah wanted to provide solutions instead of problems. The next step for finalizing Miah's move into manager was for Andie to approach the leadership team to advocate for the change, including a discussion about compensation for the new role. Miah had done the research and determined the market value of the role and provided talking points for Andie to bring to the meeting.

Although none of it was explicitly requested, all of the work Miah had done up to this point had been gladly accepted. And now, apparently the research on compensation was a step too far. There was no time to dwell on this; Miah had to get in and do a presentation, one she was already feeling anxious about! She shot a text back to Andie quickly:

> So sorry, you are totally right. I got carried away and stepped over the line. Going into my presentation but I will stop in to see you when I get to the office.

Andie's response:

> OK.

Really?! No, "Oh, right, good luck!" or, "Hope it goes well"? Miah tried to refocus and shake off her nerves as she entered the lecture hall.

By the end of the month, the new title and job description had been approved and Miah took on the new level of responsibility as manager. She was not, however, given the salary for which she had advocated—she was given the bottom of the range for managers, and on top of that, she was not given the bonus she knew the other managers had received upon signing. Even so, she assumed she would be held to the same expectations. Despite this inequity, she was glad the title was there—it would still give the program more validity. She hoped.

While Miah believed that having the title of manager would protect the program in the long term, she also knew it couldn't be her forever role. This role required her to increase her in-person time to five days a week. It was well known that Miah lived a good distance from the hospital, and with a commute of at least an hour on the best days, this was simply going to be unsustainable for more than a year. She knew, going into it, that accepting this role would officially start the countdown until she would have to leave Sinclair Hartwell.

As she worked to anticipate how long she could hold out—hopefully long enough to leave the program in a good way—she tried to extend her tenure as much as possible through requests for some flexibility. However, any requests for work-from-home arrangements for the administrative portion of her role were denied because Andie "didn't want to set a precedent."

On top of that, the unpredictable and dismissive interaction over text with Andie as the details of her role were formalized had definitely left a distinctly bad taste in Miah's mouth. It was truly shocking how quickly Andie was able to shame her for her ideas. The confidence she had been feeling in the role and all the successes she had seen were knocked away with just a single line. She was completely destabilized.

Only a few weeks after accepting this new role, Miah set a target for leaving: the end of the next calendar year. She would continue to build and support her team and work to set them up for ongoing success when she left.

Miah's working relationship with Andie continued on a bumpy path, and those bumps eventually bled into other parts of the job as well.

Social Capital

Miah recognized early on in her work at Sinclair Hartwell the importance of social capital—being a good colleague and acknowledging people for their contributions to the work. While she could have focused only on her SUDR team, she instead worked hard to build a personal connection with the clinicians and managers across departments, the administrative staff, and perhaps most importantly, the maintenance staff. She prided herself on building a community involved in contributing to every aspect of the work. Within Miah's locus of control, and in her role as a team leader, she was able to build a strong culture among staff. What she soon realized was that if her own supervisor—the person who was ultimately responsible for the success of the team—was not aligned and didn't share her values, her efforts would be unsustainable.

Miah worked hard for four years to build valuable social capital across the institution. A significant part of what Miah's work ethic encouraged her to do was be available, collegial, collaborative, and kind. She prioritized spending time on relationship building. Once those relationships were built, Miah could raise concerns about a policy that was problematic and be heard, or she could tell the maintenance staff she needed help rearranging the individual meeting rooms and they would pitch in to get things done.

When Andie arrived, she slowly but surely disrupted the work environment for Miah by being divisive and undermining her social capital. One such example involved damaging a carefully curated partnership with a historically difficult peer.

When Miah first arrived at Sinclair Hartwell, the manager of the department of Youth and Family Services (YFS) had been a near constant source of aggravation for the staff in the SUDR department. She was regularly antagonistic and dismissive of their work, and she often put her colleagues down. In addition, she was involved in a close personal relationship with the director of health services for the medical center—in other words, their boss' boss. This created a power imbalance among the staff and emboldened this manager to behave in domineering ways. Once Miah took on the leadership of her department, she worked hard to mend those relationships and build trust with this peer.

A few months after Andie's arrival, when Miah was still working to maintain the improved relationships she had developed across the departments, Andie called Miah into a meeting where the YFS manager was also present. Miah had not been told what the meeting was about.

Andie started the meeting by ceding the floor to the YFS manager, who proceeded to give negative feedback about Miah's interactions with some of the YFS staff. Miah knew of the interactions to which she was referring, and she didn't feel the representation was at all accurate. She also had not heard this feedback directly before and now she was being reprimanded by a peer in front of her boss. Rather than give Miah a chance to tell her version of the events, Andie promptly interjected, asked

Miah to apologize, and stated that she would expect her not to engage in that manner again.

Miah was exhausted, both physically and emotionally, and she crumbled with the shock of Andie's response, but she kept her composure. Getting upset was something Miah never wanted to do in front of either her own supervisor or this particular colleague, due to their tenuous history. At that moment, Miah felt all the work she had done to build bridges with the YFS staff had been dismantled. Her social capital was crumbling at the hands of her own manager who was supposed to be on her side. The power had shifted squarely out of her control and into the hands of a woman who had been historically antagonistic and had strong relational power at the hospital overall.

Power, Control, and Isolation

Andie's role at Sinclair Hartwell was Director of the Division of Behavioral Health. As the director of a division, one's leadership style and communication style—both how and with whom one communicates—becomes, over time, the culture of the team. The culture had been collaborative and collegial prior to Andie's arrival.

Miah had been working closely with one of the more experienced and forward-thinking staff members, Julie, who held a doctoral degree and was an internationally known crisis intervention specialist with a whole host of accolades. While Julie didn't manage her own team and was technically a client-facing service provider herself, Julie's position reported into the division director and worked across all departments. Miah and Julie got along well and were in strong alignment as to how to move programs forward. When Andie arrived as director, she behaved in a way that suggested she felt threatened by Julie and the other more senior staff members. Almost 20 years younger than many department staff, Andie became known to dismiss contributions from the more tenured members and started making changes that frustrated the staff.

Andie's actions potentiated the departure of a number of long-term staff, whom she quickly replaced with junior and inexperienced staff. Elevating younger women was clearly part of Andie's vision. But in a healthcare setting, this has to be done with great care. People don't stop having complicated issues, difficult relapses, and other significant needs to give you time to grow and develop a new staff.

At the same time, Andie introduced some changes that disrupted the positive relationships Miah had built. For example, she physically separated Miah from Julie by moving Miah's office to another floor, which, incidentally, also reduced Miah's accessibility to her team. She also changed the reporting structure so that Julie, 25 years Andie's senior, was no longer reporting directly to Andie but to a manager of one of the departments. This was viewed by all as a symbolic demotion of an incredibly talented staff member. In making these two moves, Andie diminished the power Julie had previously held as a longtime and expert contributor to the work, and the collective power that comes with collaboration and community.

Miah suddenly felt isolated and certainly lost the momentum she had gained by building a community of colleagues who were aligned in the ways their work could be improved.

Miah Is Silenced

Despite her frustration, Miah continued in her efforts to be a positive influence at Sinclair Hartwell. She maintained her high standards of excellence and did what she could to influence decisions that would be aligned with the hospital's stated mission and previously earned accolades.

As a manager and the senior-most expert on substance use disorders and addiction at the hospital, Miah was often invited to department meetings where options were considered and policy changes were discussed. Andie attended the meetings as well. Miah had gotten used to using her voice to share her knowledge and that had been welcomed and encouraged by the department. After Andie had made her mark on the team dynamics, destroying Miah's social capital and isolating her from colleagues who supported her work, she began to show displeasure when Miah spoke up. She would often disregard her input as if she hadn't spoken at all. In one meeting, however, she went a step further. During the meeting, Andie sent a text to Miah:

> You need to stop talking now. I see what you are doing here and I don't appreciate it.

Miah sat there stunned and thought, *Why am I even here if I can't contribute my expertise?*

There Had Been Signs

When Miah thought about the text-shaming incident from the day of her presentation and the other challenges she faced along the way, she recalled a concerning interaction the first time she met Andie.

During the hiring process, when Andie had been selected as the finalist for the director position, Miah was invited to participate in a group interview. There were nine people on the interview team, and they had a total of 30 minutes with the candidate.

At one point during the interview, Andie made a comment that made Miah very uncomfortable. She said, "My passion is for helping those who can't help themselves, for protecting the innocent. While recovering addicts certainly need, and will continue to receive, our support, there is a certain responsibility they must take for their condition."

At the time, Miah had been concerned. But when Andie got the job, she had to let go of her worries and hope for the best. Reflecting on that interaction nearly a year later, she considers that it was, in fact, a sign of how supportive Miah should have expected Andie to be of her work.

And now that she's seen how Andie has shown up in this role, she knows just how significant this first interaction had been as a backdrop to Miah's experience. With the knowledge of Andie's true personal feelings about substance use, regardless of what she professed to be her professional take, it was hard for Miah not to feel like her job, her team, and her life's work was on rocky ground. She had been trying to build a culture of community and support across all of the behavioral health departments. Knowing the person responsible for the existence of that work could be persuaded to believe it was less important did a lot of damage to her own motivation, let alone her ability to build a strong culture in the workplace.

From the Outside Looking In: Toxic Culture at Sinclair Hartwell Medical Center

As we reflect on Miah's situation, we can't help but notice some of the aspects of toxic work culture that were evident, even in this small excerpt of her overarching experience.

- Miah experienced **abusive behavior** from her manager.

- Andie was **unpredictable,** catching Miah off guard with comments that **minimized Miah's worth** and contributions.

- Andie **abused her power** in a number of ways that affected Miah either directly or indirectly.

- Andie consistently **minimized and dismissed the experience or expertise** of the long-tenured staff members.

- She **isolated people** to break up relationships that she felt were working against her.

- She **undermined her staff** in front of other leaders.

All of these actions led to a **lack of trust and psychological safety** on the team.

More broadly, there were some indicators of toxic culture at Sinclair Hartwell. Specifically, there was a possible **conflict of interest** and an extreme **lack of professionalism** exhibited through the existence of close personal relationships across levels of authority within the same division of the hospital.

Overall, **lack of trust** is the element that shines most brightly in Miah's experience. She thought she was working together with Andie to move the program forward, but she soon realized that all of their efforts were being made in opposition to one another.

 Before reading about Briana, take a moment in the companion journal to process Miah's situation.

 Chapter 5

Briana's Honeymoon Is Over

Let's resume Briana's story where we left off in Chapter 2. Recall that Briana was heading back to work after returning from a trip to Jamaica to visit her parents. Her first few months had been a learning experience. She discovered her boss had high standards and was pretty demanding, but Briana was energized by the work and had been working hard to build a level of trust with Linda. While a few things had happened that were worrisome, Briana had enough experience to know the first few months of any new job can be unsettling.

As we step back into Briana's story, tune into the elements of power, trust, and psychological safety that Briana is (or is not) experiencing. At the end of this chapter, we will take a step back and discuss some of the toxic behaviors we see.

Blindsided

Briana walked into the office and was greeted with a warm welcome. In her typically energetic way, Linda asked about Briana's trip, her parents, how her daughter handled the flights, and how she was dealing with the time change. Then they dove into the work. Linda updated Briana on what was on the plate for the week and let her know how much she was missed while she was out. She shared two main updates: the leadership team was continuing to work on a big project that required a lot of in-person work time, and the new executive that was hired back in December, Karen, was struggling without administrative support. Linda asked Briana to lean in and support Karen with calendar management while they searched for a longer term administrative support solution.

Briana immediately dove into working through some conflicts on Linda's schedule to make room for the weekly work sessions with the leadership team. Linda also needed additional one-on-one meetings with every leadership team member during the following week. What a mess it was—so much to squeeze onto an already full calendar! And now adding Karen's calendar to the mix, Briana was feeling squeezed herself.

As her first week back progressed, Briana felt like she'd been thrown back to day one. She had worked so hard to get to know Linda and her preferences and to learn the context of the work from Linda's perspective. Now she was being asked to learn a whole new person's preferences and workload. And, of course, as the CEO, Linda didn't want to see a reduction in her level of support in order to make room for the support Karen needed.

Whatever this project was that the leadership team was working on, it must have been intense! It required so much meeting time, and the project had kicked off back in early November, just a month after Briana had started. The operations manager had been running the project along with two outside consultants, so luckily, Briana didn't have to worry herself with the content of the meetings or any of the prep, other than ordering meals.

One particularly busy day at the office, Briana was trying to figure out an urgent thorny issue with Linda's calendar. As she often did, she looked for the operations manager to problem solve with her. As she approached the conference room to interrupt her, Linda rushed up and grabbed her. "No, don't go in there! She is on a series of calls and is letting the members of her team go."

Briana stood in disbelief. *What? What do you mean she is letting her team go?* Her face must have shown the shock she was feeling because Linda brought her back to their desks and explained there was a huge reduction in force being rolled out today. Briana herself was safe, but a number of people would be losing their jobs. There would be a call for the whole organization to attend at the end of the day to share the news.

Blindsided was the only way to describe Briana's feelings at that moment. She was the executive assistant to the CEO. She was supposed to be her trusted confidante. She had proven herself reliable and dependable through her first three months, keeping information close to her chest. Why had she not been trusted with this information, or even provided just a few days of advanced notice? Was this the big project that had been in the works for the last two months? While she completely understood the need to carefully roll out news like this, she was struggling with how she was supposed to continue to develop this trusting relationship with Linda when something this big had been kept from her until the last minute.

She thought about all of the scheduling changes since she returned from her trip, and suddenly it was all clear. She couldn't help but wonder, though, whether she would have approached them differently had she been given this context. Linda had been asking her to be more proactive and less reactionary—asking her to operate more independently. But now she felt rattled. How was she supposed to make independent decisions about Linda's priorities if she was going to keep something this significant from her?

The next day, Linda met with Briana to talk about how the layoffs would impact her. A few of the people Briana worked with closely would be leaving, so there would definitely be some tasks she would have to take on and some kinks to work out. So much for feeling solid in her job.

Supporting Another Executive

While the news of the layoffs came as a shock, the addition of Karen was also taking its toll on Briana. Karen's style was different from Linda's. And she had a lot going on. She also had an enormous team who demanded a lot of her time, her role involved site visits to the various youth centers, and she owned some huge projects that required uninterrupted thinking time. To top it all off, she lived within the region of the GLY community, but on the far edge of it—meaning that travel to the central office for in-person meetings took a good deal of her time. It didn't take long for Briana to realize that Karen actually needed her own dedicated administrative assistant.

Meanwhile, Linda continued to expect all she had expected from Briana before the layoffs and before taking on Karen's administrative support. She acknowledged it was a lot and indicated an openness to feedback: "Please tell me if you are overwhelmed or if it's too much." Briana didn't want to admit it, but it was. She was making some mistakes she otherwise would have been able to avoid, and some tasks were slipping through the cracks.

Before things spiraled out of control, she raised the white flag to Linda. In one of their daily check-ins, Briana admitted, "It's a lot to be supporting you and Karen. I feel overwhelmed." Linda's response was sympathetic, "Oh, I know it is. Just hang on. It's just until we hire someone for Karen." And then she returned to the agenda.

That's not the response Briana was looking for. She was hoping Linda would work with her to remove some items from her plate and to prioritize her list so she could do better work. Frustrated, Briana let it go. But she brought it up again two weeks later after Linda had expressed disappointment in two more calendar errors and a missed communication. Briana got the same response. "It's only for a little while longer."

Briana was frustrated. She was failing at the job she was hired for, but not because she was incapable of doing it well; rather, she was being asked to do far more than what should have been expected.

No Boundaries

In the midst of all of this chaos, Briana was doing her best to be a good mother. She tried to maintain some boundaries in the evening, checking her email for anything urgent but not replying outside of business hours. She was already leaving for work before her daughter was awake, so she wanted to ensure she had evening time to spend with her.

One day at the office, Briana got a call from daycare saying her daughter wasn't feeling well. She left to take her to the pediatrician, and 24 hours later they were in the pediatric intensive care unit (PICU). Briana's daughter had an underlying medical condition that resulted in increased risk with any respiratory illness.

On the first day of the illness, Linda expressed deep concern for Briana and what she was going through. "Do what you need to do, and keep me posted." She emailed the leadership team to let them know Briana would be out for a while and to come directly to Linda with questions that would usually go to Briana.

Once checked in to the PICU, however, Briana wasn't sure where she stood. Even though Linda had said she should "do what she needed to do," Briana's phone rang on schedule for their daily check-in. Linda inquired about Briana's daughter and then asked, "So, what do you want to do here? Are you taking PTO or are you working from the hospital?" Briana felt the sudden pressure of a decision—a decision she wished hadn't been put on her shoulders. She hadn't spent any time thinking about work—she had been too worried about her daughter. So she fumbled with her response and said, "I guess I can try to work from here as much as I can."

As it turned out, that was a mistake. The week in the hospital was incredibly stressful. Doctors in and out, all while a flurry of emails, texts, and phone calls came through. Sometimes the doctors' rounds would overlap with when Linda wanted to talk to Briana, or Briana would get on the phone thinking it was a quiet time, and then nurses would come to check on her daughter. Briana was being expected to be fully present both at work and in the hospital, and it wasn't working.

The following week, Briana returned to the office and Linda was over the moon with excitement to have her back. Briana never got to address the personal invasion she had felt because she was right back in the hot seat from the minute she returned.

Summer was rolling around the corner, and Briana couldn't wait. She was barely holding on. By this time, she had transitioned Karen's administrative support to a new assistant, but the damage had been done. Mistakes had occurred during that overwhelming time and Linda brought them up time and time again. The confidence that Briana had felt returning from her trip in January was shattered. She questioned her own ability to do the job and she worried about almost every interaction with Linda. She needed a break in the worst way. Thankfully, the whole organization shut down for the first week of July for "summer close." With everyone off, she would truly get a break. It couldn't come fast enough.

From the Outside Looking In: Toxic Leadership at GLY

Briana's experience centered mostly on her manager, who was also the most senior person at the organization, and illustrated some of the classic **abuse of power and narcissistic leader behaviors**.

Early on, Briana experienced constantly **shifting expectations**. Although she thought she would be part of a team, she was **isolated** physically in the office. She was told her workday started at 9, but then was expected to arrive at 8:30, as if that had been the expectation all along.

Linda demonstrated a **lack of trust** in Briana, even after Briana had spent months developing a strong trusting relationship with her. **Information was being withheld** from Briana that impacted her ability to do her job well. Then, when Linda was upset at the way things were handled, she **rewrote her version of history** and expected Briana to have been operating with the benefit of all of the knowledge.

Briana's **concerns were dismissed** repeatedly and her **perspective was invalidated**. After **raising concerns and then being ignored**, when those circumstances resulted in a mistake, Briana was **held responsible**. It was never acknowledged that she had predicted this might happen. Even after her mistakes were addressed, she was **reminded** of them, time and time again.

 Before reading about Evelyn, take a moment in the companion journal to process Briana's situation.

 Chapter 6

Evelyn's Heroes Fall From Greatness

Here we return to Evelyn's story as she starts her first day in the office after moving into her simple, shared apartment in San Francisco. Recall that Evelyn has taken on a part-time role with the organization she interned with during graduate school. And while she's passionate about the work, she's nervous about finances. But more than anything, she is thrilled to be working with such iconic feminist leaders.

As you read Evelyn's story, consider the elements of toxic culture that shape her experience. At the end of this chapter, we will take a step back and discuss some of the toxic behaviors we see.

Rocky Start

Evelyn could only be described as an eager go-getter. She was so excited about the important work Rise was doing. She was thrilled to be given the program associate role, especially at a time when some of her classmates were struggling to get jobs in their field. Having grown up in Belgium, Evelyn was fluent in French, which was of tremendous value to the organization, given their work with French-speaking African nations.

To supplement her part-time income, Evelyn took on a waitressing job at a local restaurant. This meant working evenings and weekends on top of her daytime hours at Rise, so the schedule was demanding. But every time rent was due or she had to restock the kitchen, she knew that having a second job was unavoidable. Just as the exhaustion really started to sink in, Evelyn heard rumblings at the office about funding shortages.

So now, on top of the low part-time salary and the exhaustion of waiting tables instead of sleeping, there was added instability about the future of Rise.

Just when Evelyn was about to give up and ask the restaurant about coming on full time, Rise landed a major grant. The atmosphere at the office was like a New Year's Eve celebration. They popped a bottle of champagne pulled from the back of a closet and the whole team joined in the toast. The important work they had begun would continue!

With this new injection of funds, the bosses wanted Evelyn to transition to full time. She had proven herself valuable in her first few months and they would love to have more of her time. This was a no-brainer, of course, because Rise provided the work she wanted to be doing with her degree; she did not go to years of school to wait tables. While the salary for the full-time role was not enough to make Evelyn relax completely, it was better than what she was making part time.

The organization still was not offering health benefits to their employees—they were all paid as consultants with 1099 status. Once she gave up her waitressing job, she wouldn't be making that much more money and she still would have to cross her fingers she would not get sick, but at least she would be working *one* job instead of two jobs with conflicting schedules.

Around the same time that Evelyn was considering the full-time offer, her work visa was set to expire. Rise had already sponsored her work visa when she was initially hired and was set up to do so again. Just knowing she didn't have to work to convince a different employer to be her sponsor was enough to solidify Evelyn's decision to accept the role. She gave up the waitressing job and shifted to full-time program associate.

Despite the worries and the financial challenges, she was still so grateful for the opportunities this work provided and for the support she was getting as a young woman navigating work in a new country.

The Elephant in the Room

Evelyn was not alone in her financial struggles though. Of the small group of employees at Rise, many were in the same situation as Evelyn: young and enthusiastic but struggling to make ends meet and support themselves. Three of her colleagues were married to investment bankers or tech entrepreneurs, and she noticed how they didn't carry the weight of the world on their shoulders.

Outside of the executive director, whose compensation was unknown to the team, no one was paid "well"—certainly not enough to live in an expensive city on their own without financial worry.

There was something ironic about this particular team within Rise being one in which most of the women doing the work were struggling to support themselves: struggling to pay rent, living paycheck to paycheck to make ends meet in an expensive city, and hoping to stay healthy without health insurance.

Evelyn's programs at Rise focused on housing and domestic violence. She and her colleagues spent their days advocating for a woman's right to safe housing and their ability to own property. They worked on showing the connection of these issues to the prevalence of domestic abuse. All of this work was research-based and fundamental to women's basic human rights of safety and security.

On the one hand, the young women on her team were constantly reminded of "just how bad it could be" and to be grateful they lived in a country where safety and security were theoretically available to all women. And at the same time, they were all struggling to make ends meet. They were forced into housing in neighborhoods that were less safe because that's all they could afford, and they weren't able to save money with the hopes to one day be able to own their own property.

This dichotomy was not addressed in any sort of open forum. The main response to any concern raised was some form of "you should be grateful, it could be much worse." So Evelyn just kept trying to remind herself of that.

Blurred Lines

The atmosphere in the Rise office felt very casual—almost familial. The office itself was in a house, so moving about the office felt a little bit like moving around your aunt's house with your siblings and your cousins. It felt the opposite of corporate, which was initially inviting to the young women who were drawn to work there. Team meetings held around a conference room table that felt more like a dining room table elicited a holiday meal vibe. And meetings always started with a check-in question, providing an opportunity to get to know each other as people as well as colleagues.

This familial feel was great at first, but the deeper into her work she dove, Evelyn noticed some concerning signs, and soon interactions in the office crossed a more obvious line. There were comments and questions about the way young women looked and how they dressed. Sometimes it was even connected to the conversation around money and the salary adjustments young women were advocating for. Offhanded comments were tossed around like, "Isn't that a nice bag? I guess you don't need a raise after all."

There were even comments laced with sexual innuendo: "Are you tired because you were out late with *you know who*? Wink, wink." Occasionally, one of Evelyn's peers would speak up and say she was uncomfortable with a comment or an interaction.

But raising that concern was met with a reminder that the leaders at Rise were iconic feminists, that they had fought in the '70s for women's rights.

They would brush it off and say, "It's a joke. We're all family here," or, "This isn't a typical workplace. We're allowed to say these things because we are not operating under the patriarchy."

As these incidents ramped up and Evelyn's comfort level with the internal dynamics of Rise grew more and more unstable, one of her colleagues at the associate level was asked to go to a fundraising meeting. It wasn't normal for associates to go to meetings with funders, but it was quite clear why she was being asked. The boss approached her and said, "We need you to go talk to this man and get us the grant. I'm too old, and you're the young, pretty, blonde thing—so go get us that money!"

As a young woman with little work experience, Evelyn was shocked by what she was witnessing. She had to believe that had a man said this to a young woman in the workplace, there would be a valid harassment charge. How was this behavior happening here of all places?

On almost a daily basis, Evelyn navigated shifting, conflicting feelings about Rise. It was ostensibly an epic place for women and advocacy for women's rights, and yet, at any point, the very feminism that fueled their good work might be flipped against her.

From the Outside Looking In: Toxic Environment at Rise

Evelyn's experience centered around **lack of professionalism** in the workplace, but she also experienced **abuse of power** from the leadership.

From the beginning, the office culture was informal and "familial." This caused a **lack of boundaries** when it came to defining appropriate and inappropriate communication. Evelyn and her peers felt their **personal and professional lives were entwined**, with their colleagues **using information about their personal lives "against" them**.

There was a **constant feeling of insecurity** by the employees at Rise. They were struggling to support themselves, they worried about what would happen if they got sick, and the work environment fluctuated from celebrations with champagne to panic about whether they would get another donation.

Leadership abused their power by **dismissing concerns** brought up by employees, or by making assumptions about how employees were choosing to spend their meager income. The **dismissiveness** spanned the breadth of concerns raised—from advocating for a raise to reporting an offensive comment or behavior in the office. To make matters worse, they used the plight of the women they served against their employees with a constant refrain of **"you should be grateful."**

A common theme throughout Evelyn's experience was her relative youth. Along with most of her peers, she was at the beginning of her career. They had **nothing to compare their experience to.** So while Evelyn was uncomfortable with a lot of what was going on, she truly wasn't sure whether it was "normal" or not. The leadership **took advantage of their naiveté.**

 Before reading about Nina, take a moment in the companion journal to process Evelyn's situation.

 Chapter 7

Nina's Kindness Is Not Reciprocated

This chapter picks up Nina's story as she was about to embark on the yearlong cohort of the American Equity Corps (AEC). Nina felt good about her first three years at PArts and was proud of the work they were doing to support arts access for youth in underserved communities. As a proud Latina, she was looking forward to bringing equity learning back to the organization.

As Nina navigates her year of participation in the AEC as a representative of PArts, note the elements of toxic culture that are present. At the end of this chapter, we will take a step back and dive into some of the toxic behaviors we see.

Extending Humanity in Times of Crisis

Nina and Jade were ready to get started. They had met with the executive director of PArts and Simone, the colleague who seemed to be "in charge" of the organization's AEC participation—although it wasn't clear to Nina why that was. They worked to understand the organizational expectations, which included Nina and Jade engaging fully in the AEC activities as participants and learners. This would require attendance at quarterly weeklong virtual professional development sessions and mentoring sessions in between. The mentoring was to be done by organization, so Jade and Nina would meet together with a mentor. Then, following each session, they would turnkey their learning for the full organization at PArts' in-person retreats.

As Nina and Jade were preparing for the first AEC session, Jade received some devastating news. Her father had passed away suddenly. As an organization, PArts had historically been incredibly humane when employees were faced with personal crises. Jade immediately headed home to be with her family. A communication was shared with the full organization so everyone would know she would be out of office indefinitely and that she was suffering and should be treated gently upon her return. Her work was covered by colleagues or put on hold.

As Jade and Nina had not yet worked together much, they were just beginning to get to know one another. Nina immediately swung into action and took on all of the prep responsibilities for the first AEC meeting. She let Jade know when she returned to work a few weeks later that all she had to do was show up—she had taken care of everything else.

What Nina didn't realize at the time was how long she would be covering for Jade. Even after Jade had resumed her regular projects at PArts, Nina still found herself bearing the brunt of the AEC work. When it came to preparing to present what they had learned to the entire PArts organization, Jade and Nina would meet, and Nina would end up handling all the next steps, while Jade would pop in and give feedback or make a single slide. Nina was starting to feel an imbalance in their partnership, but she also felt sorry for all Jade had gone through personally, so she let it go.

Navigating Unnamed Power Dynamics

As Nina and Jade (but mostly Nina) navigated the AEC, PArts continued to roll out their third organizational transition in four years. As a part of their equity work, they had restructured the organization to eliminate most of the existing hierarchy. While this was designed to create a balance of power, along with it came a lack of clarity.

Nina's first experience with this lack of clarity was regarding the role Simone had played in selecting Nina and Jade for the AEC and setting expectations for their work. Simone had no formal, transparent role, so Nina wasn't sure whether she should talk to her about her concerns or not.

Generally, it was a confusing time at PArts. Everybody's roles were shifting and the power dynamics were weird. The outward message was "nobody has power or authority over anybody else; nobody 'reports' to anyone in the traditional sense," but that didn't seem to help the confusion.

During this time, PArts hired an HR associate to support the director of human resources. As it turned out, the new associate was a longtime personal friend of Jade, and Jade's behavior toward Nina shifted almost immediately. She became more emboldened in her treatment of Nina as the "worker bee" of the partnership. She gave her directives and continued to do little of the work required for the AEC.

Nina also noticed that, more and more, Jade was gossiping about colleagues at the organization. She was becoming increasingly uncomfortable in the partnership with Jade, but she didn't know where to turn.

Because of the new organizational structure, she didn't have a traditional manager to go to for support. The only person with clear authority was the executive director of the organization, a position that felt too out of reach for Nina; she didn't think she needed to bring her concerns "to the top." HR was most certainly not a safe space for her anymore, so Nina ultimately felt she had no choice but to continue to keep her concerns to herself.

Promotions Are Complicated

Nina was buoyed through all of these challenges on the recognition she received from a few of her colleagues. The director of HR, the executive director, and Nina's former manager had noticed all the work she had been taking on, and they approached her about a promotion. They would have to rewrite her job description to include increased responsibilities, of course, but they wanted to recognize her contributions to the company.

As a result, Nina embarked on a lengthy effort to rewrite her job description while continuing to navigate a complicated power dynamic with Jade. This required multiple drafts, line edits, and lots of time. At long last, it was ready and approved, but then

Nina was told to keep it quiet. The justification was that it would raise too many questions if there was an announcement—too many questions about the new organizational structure, too many questions about how others could earn promotions.

While Nina was grateful for the promotion, this behavior felt odd, as her experience with PArts so far had been one of great camaraderie and celebration. She recalled numerous times when colleagues were celebrated widely, through emails, announcements at all-team meetings, or toasts at a rare team dinner.

Toward the end of the AEC year, a critical role in the organization became vacant. Nina heard rumblings that Jade was being considered for the role, which brought up concerns. This role was central to the functioning of the organization, and while it didn't have explicit decision-making authority, she could imagine Jade approaching it in the same way she had approached her relationship with Nina—from a position of assumed power. She also had concerns about Jade's tendency to gossip and her friendship with the HR associate.

The position was posted and multiple people from within the organization applied. Jade got the role, giving the appearance that it had been a foregone conclusion. Because it was such a major move, Jade's new role couldn't be kept a secret—and indeed, it was celebrated.

To make matters worse, Jade took Nina's work from the AEC and presented it as her own, as a platform for how she was going to approach her new role. This was getting hard for Nina to watch.

And still, no announcement or acknowledgement about Nina's own promotion.

Nina was beginning to feel incredibly isolated and lonely. She had no one she trusted, and it was about to get worse. When Simone scheduled a meeting with her, the last year suddenly became clear. Simone was being tapped to move into the executive director role when the current leader stepped down in a few months. Clearly this had been in the works for some time, as it explained Simone's role in setting up the expectations for the AEC and her presence in "leadership" decisions despite the flat organizational structure.

In that meeting, Simone shared something that rocked Nina's confidence. She told her that she did not approve of the promotion Nina had been given and that she had not been a part of the decision-making process. She also referred to a few things about Nina's personal life that Nina knew she had only shared with Jade during their work on the AEC. It was clear Jade was talking to Simone about Nina, and Simone was about to be the senior-most leader of the organization. Nina felt her own position at PArts was tenuous at best.

What Is Happening Here?

After the secret promotion, Nina had been given permission to hire a communications associate to support the marketing work. It had been a hard year for Nina as she bore the burden of the AEC, took on additional responsibilities without anyone's knowledge, and navigated tricky relationships. The associate was a godsend, and she enjoyed working with her.

After just three months, seemingly out of nowhere, Simone approached Nina and told her that she had to let her one associate go. She gave no explanation, just that they had to cut personnel and her associate was considered extraneous. This was incredibly confusing to Nina, but with the lack of confidence caused by the meeting with Simone, she felt she had no choice but to comply with the directive.

Nina sat with her confusion and tried to make sense of it. The year had started with Nina being asked to represent the organization publicly and willingly supporting a grieving teammate. Now that individual had assumed Nina's work as her own, had obvious relational power in the organization, and was being celebrated after a year in which Nina had witnessed an incredible lack of professionalism. Simone was poised to take over as senior-most leader, and all Nina's interactions with her for the last year had been uncomfortable at best.

Nina was starting to think about leaving PArts, but she was worried about how she would be perceived. When an organization goes through a tremendous effort to increase representation and move people of color into positions of power, departures can often signal a lack of support. As a White-presenting Latina, this is the last message Nina wanted to send. She was unhappy, but it had nothing to do with those changes—she was philosophically aligned with the direction PArts was moving. Nina suppressed her discomfort to avoid a misunderstanding.

From the Outside Looking In: Toxic Team-mates at PArts

Nina's experience demonstrates the effect that **lack of transparency** can have on team culture; it shows that trust can be shattered when decisions are not clear and when **power structures are hidden**. In addition, her experience begins to reveal the negative effect of **inconsistency** in the way employees are treated.

With the new structure at PArts, **decision-making authority and power was hidden**. Nina's relationship with Simone was **built on uneven terms**—Nina was not privy to the knowledge that Simone was to become the new executive director and that she might have a comprehensive view of all that was happening at the organization. Nina assumed (as she was told to assume) Simone had access to as much information as Nina herself did.

Jade's power was not structural or even formal, but the **relational power** that came with her friendship with the new HR associate emboldened her to act in a way that **minimized Nina's experience and contribution**. Nina saw Jade behave in ways that were **unprofessional**, and yet not only was she not held accountable, but **she was celebrated**.

After Simone's role in the organization became clear to Nina, **the power dynamic made Nina feel unsafe and unsure of herself**. Simone **diminished her accomplishments** by telling her **she hadn't approved of her promotion**. Psychological safety was most certainly not present for Nina—she immediately felt as if **any problem she raised would be held against her**.

 Before reading about Faith, take a moment in the companion journal to process Nina's situation.

Faith's Rocky Hike to the Glass Cliff

In Chapter 2, we learned about Faith's bumpy start to her teaching career and how it framed her approach to leadership. We left Faith's story at the pivotal moment in which Faith sent an email to welcome her newly hired deputy superintendent and executive assistant. This chapter begins with more context about Faith's decision-making process to accept the board's offer and describes her first few months in the role.

Look for the cues in Faith's story that point to how the toxicity all around her may very well be pushing her toward the "glass cliff." At the end of this chapter, we will take a step back and discuss some of the toxic behaviors we see.

The List

As a Black woman taking on a leadership role in education, Faith knew she had to navigate her career path with great care. Despite there being more women in the field of education overall, proportionally far fewer women make it to the senior-most leadership positions. The statistics for Black women are more staggering. There would be a lot on the line for Faith if she took on this role—she carried the entire community of Black women on her shoulders each and every day.

Additionally, Faith knew the evidence for female leaders—she had read all the research on the "glass cliff." The glass cliff is a social construct in which women are more likely to be asked to lead when organizations are in crisis. Because they are finally being given the opportunity to lead, they accept the risky position. The problem, of course, is that leading in a crisis has a lower chance of success than leading a mostly functional organization. As a result, the celebratory "shattering the glass ceiling" becomes the incredibly dangerous "hovering on the edge of the glass cliff."

With all the risk that was inherent in this decision as a Black woman, Faith had to make sure she thought it through completely. One of Faith's trusted mentors once had given her a piece of advice that stuck. "When considering a new role, make your list. What is the list of things you need to be successful in that role? Do you have those things? If so, go for it! If not, think twice."

Faith had thought about her list in considering taking on the interim superintendency.

1. Trust

2. Resources

3. A healthy team

She had trust. She had earned that over the years, being seen as the firefighter of the district. She was trusted by the board, trusted by her peers, trusted, in fact, by everyone in the district. Resources weren't an issue. The district had strong financial reserves, and from her perspective, decisions about how to spend those resources had been made with great care. A healthy team? Well, that was yet to be seen, but the addition of her own deputy and EA would help, and she wasn't opposed to replacing some members of the team if she needed to. So, Faith had checked all of the items on her list and taken the leap.

The Board

The first few months of Faith's tenure as interim superintendent was a period of intense listening and learning. From her new position, she asked a lot of questions and dug deep to get answers. With this came the discovery of a lot of issues that had been covered up by the previous administration—despite Erin's claims that the district had been "left in a good place." Academic achievement was down, morale was low in large pockets across the district, and there was a growing budget issue that had been kept under wraps. Despite her deep disappointment in having put complete trust in Erin and feeling misled by her mentor, Faith leaned in and got to work.

A month after hiring her new deputy and EA, Faith prepared for her quarterly board meeting, laying out a clear message for the board. Things at RPSD were not okay. Faith had uncovered a harsh reality, most of which had been building for years but kept quiet by the responsible parties in an attempt at self-preservation. In addition, one of Faith's strongest senior leaders had left, leaving her with a fragmented, young leadership team. Personnel challenges were emerging at individual schools that had been going on for years but had also been swept under the rug. Academic results had plummeted. A political transition in the state was causing financial hardship to the district—challenges that could have been anticipated but were now taking their toll. The list went on and on. Faith shared a clear message with the board: she now knew the priorities that had to be addressed and she wasn't backing down. It was time to get to work and she would need the board's support to turn things around. Faith stopped short of telling them she had been set up, but that's how she was feeling.

The board's response to the clarity of Faith's message was troublesome.

Given the historical approach with the board, she expected that her message might catch them by surprise. Just as Faith herself had been unaware of the reality, Erin had always painted a rosy picture for the board. Meetings were glowing and positive, and they always celebrated successes. There had never been a clear indication of any issues—problems had always been tackled quietly and internally.

In her previous role as associate superintendent of operations, Faith had participated in board meetings for two years. She had raised a red flag about a crisis that was building a year prior, but then she led the team to a swift resolution. Her timely response had allowed Erin to continue to focus on the positives.

The board knew Faith as a fixer. On top of that, it was clear they had no idea about the true condition of the organization.

Given the board's history with Erin at the helm and their experience with Faith in her operations role, they expected her to jump into action without reservation. "She gets it done. There's never any challenge too big for Faith!" But they didn't know how bad it was, and they weren't used to being asked for support. When Faith laid it all out in that meeting, they were stunned. One trustee said, "I've been on this board for 15 years, and this is the first time I'm hearing any of this." In reality, the trouble had been building for years, but it was still hard for the board to hear the truth and for them to accept they needed to lean in and be supportive of some difficult decisions.

Faith felt an edge in her interactions with the board from then on. They expected her to fix things and didn't want to have any part of it. "This is why we hired you!" A tall order, given the trouble she had inherited.

The Court of Public Opinion

Faith quickly learned the pros and cons to rising up through an organization to become the senior-most leader. Her knowledge of the staff, from the central office to the teachers, principals, and office managers in each school, was extensive. She had friends throughout the district. The news of her being named interim superintendent was widely celebrated. People came out of the woodwork to congratulate her and pledge their support.

From her first day as a teacher in Atlanta, Faith had always known she had a high moral compass when it came to professionalism. She expected people to act in a way that was consistent with that bar. In her mind, it was clear: they were there to do this work for students first, and she wouldn't tolerate bad behavior from adults.

After taking on the interim superintendency, Faith became aware of certain instances that were occurring across the district, situations of which she had previously been unaware. She learned of violations of the district's nepotism policy, inappropriate conduct on school property, and decisions that clearly prioritized adults at the expense of students.

Faith would not permit these situations to continue while she was at the helm, and she promptly began to address them. She was always kind, professional, and even-tempered in her approach as she carried the tough experience of her early days in Atlanta with her every day. It was never anything personal; she just could not let such behaviors stand.

While many colleagues celebrated her bravery for addressing these issues that were beginning to plague the district, some "friends" who were initially supportive were getting called out for poor decisions. Suddenly, they didn't think Faith was the right person for the job and they made that known in their circles.

In the court of public opinion, Faith was slipping. It turns out, people trust your leadership until it challenges their status quo.

All the trust she had worked so hard to build over the years was now beginning to crumble.

The Team

Faith's experience with the leadership team followed a similar pattern. Faith had previously been a peer to these colleagues, and she was the leader who was responsible. She was a collaborative leader and believed in shared decision making. And she was unafraid to make hard decisions if others weren't willing to do so.

Most of the team was initially supportive. They championed Faith and her desire to get down to business and start making changes. They were on her side until they realized that to support these changes, they were going to have to take a long, hard look at their own ways of doing business. While it would be privately and always come with an offer of assistance, they were going to have to be called out on things that weren't working.

Some team members flipped quickly. One particular member of the team was talented and saw herself as a great leader, able to give critical feedback and willing to make hard calls when needed. Soon after taking the role, Faith saw this colleague treating her direct reports unevenly. She would treat some with kid gloves, smoothing over critical feedback with caveats and gentle language. Others, she would simply "say the thing" and then absolve herself of any responsibility to help fix the problem she had named. In addition, she presented unfavorable decisions to her team without any personal accountability, blaming the organization, "leadership," or Faith directly. "Faith decided this. I wanted something different, but I'm not in charge."

Faith confronted her with this feedback as soon as she noticed. She told her it was something she'd like to see improve and that she'd like to support her in this area. Rather than lean in and accept Faith's help, this leader became combative, accusing Faith of not being grateful for how hard she was working. She denied any accountability for her actions, and despite their long history of working together, their relationship was forever changed. She then continued to undermine Faith's leadership with her actions.

It took longer for some team members to show their true colors. One leader in particular was an outspoken champion for Faith in her new role for the first six months. As assistant superintendent of human capital for the district, Jay had been Faith's peer for a few years. Jay had deep functional expertise in his area and presented himself as completely supportive of Faith's emergence as the next leader of the district. At the outset, Faith put all her trust in Jay. Given that many of the other leaders on the executive team were newer to their roles and needed more support, a great weight was lifted off Faith's shoulders to be able to trust in Jay.

As time went on, though, Faith began to worry that Jay had exploited her trust and was not working with her but explicitly against her. She learned through the grapevine that he was having drinks with board members and other influential people in the community regularly, and when asked, he was never up-front with Faith about these meetings. Jay seemed to be hiding something, and he certainly wasn't being the collaborative colleague he had promised to be. She began to worry that he was possibly undermining her leadership by developing these relationships, although she had no evidence to call him on it. Individuals are certainly permitted to develop their own relationships, so it was hard to call that out on its own as inappropriate. But something didn't quite feel right to Faith.

As time went on, the evidence came to bear. In a few critical personnel issues, Faith started to question Jay's decision making and became worried that he was putting the district in a tenuous legal position. She went to the board with her concerns, but was completely dismissed. Faith's worries had been warranted. Jay's clandestine happy hours had set him up to be in a position of power when an issue arose. Jay was in charge of his own narrative, with a direct line to influential people. Given the relationships Jay had established, along with their growing frustration that Faith wasn't able to quietly and independently fix all the district's problems, the board discounted Faith's perspective and dismissed the idea that there was anything to worry about when it came to Jay.

After enough of these situations had transpired and the curtain was pulled back on the reality of the situation in RPSD, it became an environment not unlike the old board game Hungry Hungry Hippos. Leadership team members were clawing for the limited pot of resources. They were arguing, "My hire is more important than your hire." As the team began to grapple with the challenges at hand, they would preach flexibility given the limited resources of public schools, but would never offer to give something up themselves. Team members came to the table prioritizing people over results and even more egregious, adults over students.

Six months into her interim superintendency, Faith came to learn that almost no one on her team was trustworthy after all.

Straddling the Fence, Heading for the Cliff

Each and every day, Faith got up to go to work, unsure of which group she was going to face. There were those she considered as her "ride or die" group because they knew she was about to make some big moves and they knew the district needed it. And there were others who had gotten away with so much for so long that once they saw her moral compass exposed, they knew they were going to be on the chopping block. This dynamic created a divide among the staff. Faith spent the majority of the first six months of the job with the knowledge that some people were sharpening their knives due to the impact the coming change would have on them personally.

Faith wasn't afraid of a challenge, of course. There were some concessions she was willing to make. When the leadership team turned on her, she thought, *I will replace them, as long as the board has my back.* But then the board faltered, wanting things to go back to a time when they had their blinders on and everything was "fine."

The worst part of all of this was that Faith wasn't spending any of her time on the work she wanted to be doing as superintendent.

She never talked about student achievement. She rarely talked about students, instruction, or results. She spent 75 percent of her time trying to present herself as a measured, visionary leader in the midst of being surrounded by people who wanted her to be successful… until they didn't.

A mid-year leadership team retreat was coming up. Faith had taken on this role thinking she had everything on "the list" and could fix anything that came her way. At this point, though, the trust had been diminished and her team broken. Faith needed this retreat to show her a way forward was possible. They were set to discuss a huge strategic move—how to address the looming financial crisis. She knew what had to be done to have any semblance of hope to get out of the mess they were in. She hoped and prayed this team could get on board with what needed to happen, that they would orient their conversation around what was best for the district versus what was best for themselves. Faith couldn't do this alone; she needed her team to stand with her.

From the Outside Looking In: Toxic Culture at RPSD

While the epicenter of many of our other friends' toxic experiences was their relationship with a senior leader or their own manager, in Faith's situation, she was the senior-most leader in her organization. Faith's experience shows how toxic culture can also impact the executive leader's ability to be successful.

Lack of trust was the main source of toxicity for Faith. Without a leadership team she could trust to show up and **own their responsibilities as well as their vulnerabilities** and mistakes and who would not cast the blame for all tough decisions in her direction, Faith could not see a way to get the larger organization behind her. When the near-unanimous support for her leadership began to crumble, the combination of these factors made Faith feel as if she couldn't win.

The relationship with the board was perhaps the most toxic of all. The **lack of formality** in their approach had the effect of **lulling Faith into a sense of safety and security**. Yet, when she started naming the hard truths and the board didn't like what they were hearing, they **used those things against her**, blaming her for the fact these problems existed rather than acknowledging they simply hadn't been paying attention for many years.

From the top of the organization to the bottom, there was a sense of **"every man or woman for themselves."** There was no sense of commitment to common goals, second in importance only to trust in building a strong and healthy team.

 Take a moment in the companion journal to process Faith's situation before moving onto Part 3.

PART III
Hitting Rock Bottom

"I keep my head down and for self-preservation just do my work ... Yet the irony is this: in my self-preservation, I'm actually destroying myself. In bottling up my unexpressed feelings, I'm making myself sick emotionally and physically."

— Gary Chapman, *Rising Above a Toxic Workplace*

🌀 Chapter 9
Toughing It Out

So far, we've seen our friends be drawn into their roles by the sense of optimism that mission-driven work provides. And we've traveled with them along the slow and painful descent into reality, where they are faced with abusive bosses, unprofessional colleagues, and situations where trust and psychological safety are absent.

Now that we are deep into our friends' stories, let's step back and consider the implications of working in a toxic environment. At this stage in their journey, our friends are mostly tolerating their conditions; some are considering leaving but haven't started the process yet.

This chapter will explore the impact a challenging work environment can have on a person. It will discuss the tendency people, particularly in mission-driven work, have to "tough it out" for the good of the mission, and it will lay out facts about the physical and emotional impact of "toughing it out."

Commitment

Remember the optimism from the beginning of our friends' stories? They felt a deep emotional connection to the mission of their organization. People who choose mission-driven work want to change the world. They want to bring opportunities to underserved communities. They want to make a positive impact on structural inequities that have kept opportunities at bay. They are often reliable, altruistic, committed, tireless, and dependable. While these characteristics are what draws them to the work, they can also become a barrier to self-care.

In Chapter 1, we explored how mission-driven work differs from other types of work. We noted that mission-driven work often elicits a personal commitment to the mission and its impact—which is generally human-centered rather than economically focused. While acknowledging the many upsides to this aspect of the work, the downside is that the job becomes more than an individual commitment; it becomes much larger than oneself.

When the job is no longer serving a person in the best way it can, the clues may be hard to see. One's instincts might immediately go to the mission itself ("I have to stick it out because this is good work we are doing") or to those the mission is serving ("How can I abandon these kids who need us so much?").

Once someone is deeply committed to their work, it is hard for them to have an objective view of a toxic work environment. A natural response is "yes, but..."

- "**Yes**, there is a lack of trust at my organization, **but** we are still doing good work for kids."

- "**Yes**, my boss is micromanaging and unpredictable and that puts me on edge, **but** look at the struggles the community is facing—how can I complain?"

Fill in that second blank with any number of reasons, but the result is the same. Often, the person experiencing the toxic situation will put the needs of the organization over their own needs.

In his book, *The Good Enough Job: Reclaiming Life from Work*, Simone Stolzoff discusses the idea of "passion professions," where jobs in industries such as nursing, education, and other mission-driven spaces are treated as a passion, almost a sacred duty. This view of the work diminishes workers' ability to call out injustices. Workers are expected to "not be in it for the money," which leads to gender disparities as many of these jobs are female dominated. As Stolzoff states:

> If we believe people make career decisions based on their passions, then it's easy to attribute wage disparities to individual choices rather than acknowledge the reality of structural injustice. [13]

As we saw, meager compensation shows up in one of our friends' stories, and certainly the idea of a passion profession applies there. Our friend Evelyn was told she should be grateful to have the opportunity to do this work—while working for an organization designed to break down gender inequities across the globe.

Stolzoff raises another reason people stay in toxic environments in a chapter entitled "Lose Yourself: On the myth that your work is your worth." All too often, people focus so much on their jobs that it becomes their entire identity; they begin to define who they are as the work they do. [14] In a culture where the first question you are asked when you meet someone is "what do you do?" it is not hard for your professional identity to overtake other aspects of your identity. People often stay in difficult work situations simply because they don't know who they would be if they left.

I can certainly relate to that as well. When I left my last full-time job, I felt a break in my identity. I realized that while I have a lot of other things that make me who I am, I often described myself first and foremost with my job. I had to retrain my brain to recognize that I am not wholly a person who is employed for some purpose by someone else. And while I probably didn't recognize it at the time, I definitely stayed in jobs longer than I should have because of this phenomenon.

Risk

But when employees in toxic work environments don't acknowledge and address the problem they are experiencing, they face significant risk. What's at stake when you ignore what's happening? Sadly, a lot: your mental health, your emotional stability, and even your physical health. And not just at work, the impact can (and will) go beyond the walls of the office.

In *Rising Above a Toxic Workplace: Taking Care of Yourself in an Unhealthy Environment*, coauthors Gary Chapman, Paul White, and Harold Myra share stories of toxic work environments across industries and provide strategies for processing and managing these situations. They describe toxic or dissonant organizations as rife with conflict, fear, and anger. "The environment causes people to have physiological responses as if they are in a fight-or-flight situation. Healthy people become ill; immune systems are less effective. Colds, flu, and stress-related illnesses such as heart attacks are more common." [15] Even so, people stay for the reasons we addressed above. One of the women profiled in this book shares her experience. Her health was declining and she knew the job was "killing her," but she had no other job prospects. After months of work to figure out a plan, she was able to leave—and her symptoms abated.

According to Dr. Ramani Durvasula, a renowned psychologist and author who specializes in helping patients heal from narcissistic abuse, plenty of anecdotal evidence shows that victims of the types of narcissistic abuse often displayed by toxic leaders develop physical ailments that don't make sense given their age and health. While complications with doing formal research on this topic exist, the evidence is there.

The physical impact can be indirect as well—when you are under the influence of an abusive manager, you may not take care of yourself, and you are more likely to sleep and eat poorly. [16]

Compounding the physical effects of narcissistic abuse, these leaders are "more likely to feel inconvenienced by your health issues—they do not like infirmity or other reminders of human frailty or mortality, and they are too selfish and impatient to engage in compassionate and sustained caregiving." [17] So, even if you attempt to prioritize self-care, your toxic manager is likely to make it difficult for you by imposing feelings of guilt, or by commenting about how your illness is making life difficult for them.

Beyond your physical health, toxic environments can impact you in other ways. Dr. Durvasula says that mental health challenges such as panic, depression, and anxiety (including social anxiety) are expected reactions to narcissistic abuse. So if an employee has an abusive boss who displays narcissistic behaviors—whether or not the boss is clinically narcissistic—the employee can expect to experience such challenges.

Dr. Durvasula also says it's important to note that these instances, the ones that come about as a result of narcissistic abuse are not mental health disorders on their own. This is an important distinction for survivors who might feel responsible for some inherent inability to "deal" with their boss, an instinct that it is somehow their fault. Certainly, if the victim has a preexisting mental health condition, it can be worsened by the impact of the toxic leader. Consider an individual who is managing a preexisting diagnosis of depression and/or anxiety and takes a new job with a narcissistic leader. One can easily see how the preexisting condition would intensify with this experience.

Dr. Chapman and his colleagues share the advice that survival might mean having to change the way you approach the work. And in many cases, that can mean turning into a person who is not your genuine self. Some of Dr. Chapman's clients shared these statements:

- "I persevered, but I noticed a change in my personality."

- "I had no idea my lack of joy had been so evident [to those around me]."

- "The truth is, I loved my job, but I didn't like the person I was becoming." [18]

And while anyone can be a victim of toxic work culture, the young and inexperienced employees are most easily blindsided by toxic leadership. If their professional identities are still form-ing, they may end up being influenced by the situation in a way that has a longer impact—cementing their own understanding of what workplaces are "supposed" to feel like. This phenomena explains how the toxic workplace has become ubiquitous.

The sad truth is that workplaces often foster narcissism by pro-moting cultures that make the toxic leader untouchable and reward high performers, even when their conduct in the work-place is harmful. [19] Research out of Ohio State University sup-ports this conclusion. A study led by Robert Lount and coau-thored by Bennett Tepper and Woohee Choi shows that employ-ees consistently let high-performing managers get away with abusive behavior—they view it as tough love as opposed to abuse. Lount had this to say on the topic:

> If employees see their boss as a successful leader,
> that seems to be incompatible with being abu-
> sive… So they label the abuse as something more
> positive, like "tough love."

Some might see the study as excusing toxic leadership, since the teams and leaders are, after all, producing results. But the authors are quick to note this is not the right conclusion.

> There is overwhelming evidence from years of re-
> search that abusive leadership is not good for em-
> ployees or organizations… In fact, other research
> suggests that successful bosses known for their
> "tough love" approach might be even more suc-
> cessful if they used more accepted management
> techniques. [20]

An oft heard piece of advice for someone struggling with toxic work culture is to set boundaries, be clear, and just put your head down and get the work done. This assumes a level of au- tonomy and choice with respect to how one spends their time. A response to this advice might be to clearly communicate that you won't be responding to emails after 6 p.m. or on the week- ends, or that you won't take on any work that isn't part of your agreed upon scope.

In the best of circumstances, this might be possible. But more often than not, this seemingly simple advice won't work. Systemic support is required for boundaries to hold. Consider these scenarios:

- Your boss tells you to take care of yourself, but then lets your work pile up and is frustrated because you took a day off to go to the doctor.

- Your manager notices you limping and suggests that yoga or physical therapy would be good for you, but continues to add to your plate, expecting everything to be done on time and to the highest standards.

- Your boss publicly encourages everyone to take their PTO (and criticizes those who don't), but calls you consistently for "emergencies" during your time off.

Boundaries are only good when they are supported by the system. Stolzoff says it best:

> If your company is understaffed, or it's the end of a quarter, or your pay is tied to your hours, [or, I would add, you have a narcissistic manager], setting a personal boundary is like trying to shield yourself from the sun with a cocktail umbrella. [21]

Implications

It is important to understand that what you are about to read in our friends' accounts, as well as what you or a loved one might be experiencing, is broadly experienced and widely researched.

It could be easy to dismiss the stories of our friends as a "single story" taken out of a broader context and thus not generalizable, or it could be easy to believe "that couldn't happen to me." Hopefully the information in this chapter helps to set a contextual frame for the experiences of our friends and the potential resulting impact on their health and well-being.

We opened Part 3 with words from relationship expert Gary Chapman sharing a quote from a client:

> I keep my head down and for self-preservation just do my work ... Yet the irony is this: in my self-preservation, I'm actually destroying myself. In bottling up my unexpressed feelings, I'm making myself sick emotionally and physically.

There is an inherent danger in "putting your head down" and ignoring the toxicity. It can make you sick—in more ways than one. We will now see how this risk plays out in our friends' stories.

 Before reading about our friends' lowest moments, head to the companion journal to reflect on what you've learned about the implications of "toughing it out."

Chapter 10

Our Friends Hit Rock Bottom

In Chapter 9, we reviewed some of the reasons it's hard for people to see the realities of the work environment at mission-driven organizations. We noted why people often stay in these roles, even when they start to experience toxic leadership. Earlier in the book, we traveled with each of our friends along the paths of discovery—where they saw the toxicity emerge in their daily experiences. But at this point in our friends' stories, while they might be thinking about leaving at some point, they are still deep in the work.

Chapter 9 also taught us about some of the dangers of maintaining exposure to toxic working conditions. Let's now return to our friends and see the impact of their experiences.

Miah's Invisible Illness

In Chapter 4, we saw all the ways the arrival of Miah's new boss had taken a toll on her work environment. All the work Miah had done previously to build team culture, to build relationships across teams, and to elevate the importance of her department was all crumbling before her eyes.

In the meantime, Miah's responsibilities at home were drawing more and more of her attention. Her daughter was finishing high school and about to move out of the country for college. Her husband had initiated a career change and suffered from a chronic illness that was once again flaring up. She wanted (and needed) to be home and present for her family—for doctor appointments, for treatments, and for the final weeks of her daughter living at home.

But Andie continually denied her requests for a day or two of working from home, even though Miah's responsibilities could be arranged to accommodate remote work. She already ran staff meetings on Zoom, as the full team was never scheduled to be on-site at a common time. She had few clinical responsibilities and could organize her week to do administrative tasks on her days from home. Yet Andie always gave the same response: "If we provide flexibility for you, we have to do it for everyone."

So Miah continued to push through, driving more than an hour in each direction, bearing the mental and emotional toll of dealing with a family illness from a distance and the guilt of not spending the last few weeks with her daughter. For necessary appointments and treatments, she took sick days.

In September, Miah took two and a half weeks of PTO to move her daughter to college. Despite the inherent stress of that activity, it truly felt like the first real vacation Miah had taken in a while. Toward the end of the time off, her body finally relaxed. Unsurprisingly, Miah got sick right before the flight home.

By the time she returned to Atlanta, all the viral symptoms had passed, but an extreme case of vertigo remained. No matter what she tried, Miah couldn't shake it. The dizziness was ever present. Under pressure to return to work, she drove to the office on her first day back. As soon as she got there, she knew it was a mistake. The vertigo was more intense and the drive had been scary. She managed to make it through the day and get home safely that night, but she told Andie she wasn't going to be able to return the next day.

Miah had enough PTO left to remain out the rest of the current week and a few days the following week. To get to the root cause of the vertigo, she went to see specialists and started physical therapy. Her doctor told her she could not drive until the vertigo was gone.

At the end of the first week, Miah reached out to Andie to let her know she couldn't come back into the hospital until she was cleared by the doctor. Andie was frustrated by this news, as there was an event happening the following week that Miah had organized. It was all set and ready to go, but Andie felt Miah should be present. She asked, "Can't your husband drive you?" Miah explained that being in a car for any distance was quite uncomfortable. In addition, her husband had his own limited set of sick days and was dealing with a chronic illness. Andie still pressured her to come in. The next week, Miah was driven to work by her husband, who had to take a day off from his job to do so. While the event took place, she sat in the corner of a room feeling incredibly nauseous and never said a word. After all, the event had been organized by Miah—it didn't require her participation.

Once Miah and her husband arrived home, they both knew the trip had taken a toll. Any improvement in symptoms was gone, and Miah was feeling worse than ever. After seeing everyone at the hospital, including her team, Miah was struck by the idea of an "invisible illness." She felt terrible, yet she looked fine. Her presence that day had also impacted her relationships with her team members. She sensed there was a general lack of understanding of just how debilitating vertigo can be, and her team wanted her back.

By the time Miah used the last of her PTO later that week, her condition had not improved enough to be able to drive. If she moved slowly enough at home, she could manage time in front of the computer, so Miah asked for a medical accommodation to work from home. As she had noted before, most of her work could be done remotely without any changes, and her team was eager to continue to have access to Miah for managerial needs. Andie denied her request once again and told Miah she would have to take short-term disability leave if she couldn't come back in person.

So that's exactly what Miah did. She completely disconnected from work and focused on her health. Taking disability leave allowed her to remove the ever-present pressure to "get better faster." Little by little, Miah saw a marked improvement.

Following her leave, Miah was due to return to work after Thanksgiving. She tried not to think about it, knowing she couldn't do anything to prepare. She didn't want to go back and had started making the connection that her vertigo may, in fact, have been stress induced. Indeed, as the day of her return approached, the vertigo returned in full force. She couldn't possibly get into a car in that state, so she extended her leave by an additional week and told Andie she would be in touch.

Briana Sees Herself Changing

In Chapter 5, we followed along as Briana's confidence crumbled and her boundaries were erased. She had been counting down the weeks to "summer close" when the entire organization would shut down across all regions for the week of July 4th. Briana had arranged to go away with her family to a cabin on a lake in Northern Minnesota, with plans to meet friends to celebrate a milestone birthday. The anticipation of that trip was getting her through the days.

At long last, the calendar read July 1. Briana packed up her family and headed to the cabin. Fresh air and relaxation, finally!

Even though all the organization's employees were off, Briana kept her email active on her phone while she was away. She was aware that as the EA to the CEO, she was expected to be available for true emergencies. But Briana left her computer at home, because any true emergency could be handled via phone. Anything else could wait until Monday. After all, it was only one week.

On Wednesday evening when she was in town for dinner, Briana checked her email and noticed a flurry of messages from Linda. Her phone service was spotty at the cabin, so she hadn't gotten the texts Linda had also sent. Before sitting down to dinner, she called Linda, who told her she needed her to schedule a meeting on her behalf. Briana said she would take care of it when she got back to the office on Monday, but Linda demanded it be done immediately. When Briana explained that not only was she out to dinner with her family, but she also hadn't brought her computer along on the trip, Linda sighed in exasperation. She said, "Briana, I need you to figure this out. Waiting until Monday is not an option."

Early Thursday morning, Briana left her husband and daughter at the lake with their friends and traveled into town to find a library with a public computer. There, she logged into her work account and reached out to the people needed at the meeting. While she waited to hear back, she grabbed a few magazines and flipped through them. Much to her relief, the responses came in relatively quickly. She finished the task and returned to her family by lunch time. Linda sent an acceptance to the meeting invitation, but didn't send Briana any other acknowledgement for her effort.

When Briana returned to work on Monday, Linda welcomed her back, said she hoped she had a good trip, and then kicked off the week with this: "I need you to understand that you are always on call. Even when the whole organization is off, you are expected to be available. You should never be traveling without your computer." Briana was baffled and speechless. How was she supposed to have any sort of work–life balance if this was the case? She wasn't simply being asked to handle emergencies; she was being asked to handle anything that was asked of her, at any time, no matter where she was or what she was doing.

After that experience, Linda's trust in Briana seemed to diminish even further. Briana's main support within the organization, the operations manager, was out on medical leave, so it was a lonely time for Briana. She felt she had no one to turn to for support, and the criticism from Linda just kept coming.

During this time, Briana also noticed another trend. Linda seemed to be "breaking down" her team one by one. She noticed one particular member of the team, an otherwise lovely and confident leader, seemed to be losing her composure as well as her sunny disposition. As her EA, Briana was privy to Linda's complaints, and Briana noticed that Linda's exasperated comments about this leader began to increase. "She's in over her head." "I don't know why she is so confused." "Here's another area where I need to lean in more than I should." And worse, Briana didn't witness Linda giving any real support to this leader—she just continued to express disappointment.

Each night on her commute home, Briana reflected on this trend. She thought of at least two other people over the last few months who had gone through similar transformations, from confident and capable to nervous and unsure. The more she saw, the more she wondered if she wanted to be a part of a place that treated people like this.

One of Briana's roles was to communicate with the GLY board of directors. She had a system that had been in place for nearly a year and there had never been any problems. She didn't always get an explicit response from the board chair's assistant, but the messages were always delivered. As such, she had stopped pushing for confirmations and hadn't yet had a problem. In late July, however, a simple communication Briana sent did not make its way to the board chair. Linda was livid. Briana tried to explain that she had followed the same procedure as she had in the past, but Linda accused her of being lazy. She couldn't see it as someone else's error because Briana should have ensured it went through. That's how any mistake was seen—even if the error could be attributed to someone else, it was always Briana's fault for not catching it and fixing it.

Following that missed communication, Linda was increasingly anxious about anything that had to do with the board. A few weeks later, the board chair was again involved in something that was pinned on Briana. He was scheduled to interview a candidate for a senior-level position, and there had been some confusion about where and when the interview would take place. Everything was sorted out in plenty of time, but afterward, he reported he didn't care for the candidate. Linda came to Briana and let her know the interview had not gone well and that it was Briana's fault due to the confusion leading up to it. "This is why we can't have mistakes."

Briana was beside herself at that point. She immediately went to the restroom and couldn't hold back her tears. How was she supposed to make it in this environment? Part of being an EA is clearing up confusion—she knew that. She had done it success-fully and still somehow a bad interview was being blamed on her "incompetence." As the tears flowed, Briana didn't recognize herself. She was not a person who cried at work. She was tough as nails and had the temperament necessary for a chaotic job with messes to clean up. But this job, Linda in particular, was turning her into someone she was not. Someone who was afraid to make a mistake. Someone who questioned her own compe-tence. Someone who was bringing her sense of self-doubt home with her every night.

Briana looked in the mirror and thought, *Who am I?*

Evelyn Is Told to "Get Over It"

In Chapter 6, we felt Evelyn's roller coaster of emotions around her work at Rise. She was so grateful to have the opportunity to do work with such a profound impact. But she was uncom-fortable with the way she and her colleagues were treated; she felt it conflicted with everything she thought they were working toward reversing. This organization was putting its heart and soul into protecting women's rights, and was simultaneously underpaying its mostly female staff, not offering medical insur-ance, and operating within an unprofessional and sometimes hostile work environment.

One of the perks of Evelyn's job was the opportunity it afforded her to travel internationally. One or two times a year, Evelyn would accompany the senior-most leaders to important diplo-macy meetings with female politicians, advocates, missionaries, and diplomats in Europe, Asia, and Africa. Her role at these meetings was primarily administrative. She supported the planning efforts from the home office and then during travel she would support set up and tear down and would take minutes at the meetings.

Two years into her time at Rise, around the height of Evelyn's uneasiness with the work culture, she had the opportunity to travel to a small African country on the northern coast. She got all the required vaccinations and prepared extensively for the trip. Once the team landed after the long flight, Evelyn was exhausted on a level she had never before experienced. She chalked it up to jet lag and did everything she could to keep up with the team.

But when she awoke the next morning, she knew she was not okay. She was so tired she could barely pick up her arms to get her phone. Her whole body ached, and she was sure she had a fever. She called her boss and let her know she thought she was sick. Given the fears about malaria and other diseases prominent in African countries, Evelyn anticipated a compassionate response. Instead, she explained her symptoms and heard a huge sigh on the other end of the line.

"Are you kidding me?" her boss said. "Do you have any idea what these women go through on a daily basis, and you are complaining about being tired and having some aches?"

Evelyn was shocked and at first was speechless. Finally she said, "I'm really sorry, but I don't think it's just being tired and having 'some aches.'"

Her boss was having no part of it. "Well, this is just so inconvenient, Evelyn. The meeting is tomorrow, and I need you there to take notes. I guess we'll set up without you today, but get over yourself and find a way to be there at the meeting tomorrow no matter what."

Evelyn hung up the phone and dissolved into tears. Even crying hurt her whole body. Once she had calmed down a bit, she did what most people who can would do when they feel terrible: she called her mom in Brussels. "Mom, I'm so sick. And my boss told me to 'get over it.' I can't do this anymore, I have to get out of this job." As much as she could from across the globe, Evelyn's mom gave her the comfort and care she needed and validated Evelyn's instinct to quit. She told her not to worry, they would work it all out when she was back in California.

The next day, Evelyn showed up at the meeting, barely able to sit upright, and took the notes as directed. Her boss didn't pay much attention to her. After a "look who decided to show up today" greeting, she certainly didn't ask how she was feeling. Evelyn watched the clock closely through the end of the day. Her only motivation was the thought that the end was in sight. *Tomorrow I will be on a plane going home. As soon as I am well enough to go back to work, I will resign.*

A Perfect Storm of Grief and Micromanagement for Nina

In Chapter 7, we followed Nina through a tumultuous year of navigating hidden sources of power. Her participation in the

America Equity Corps was no longer a true partnership. The transition to a flat organization without explicit power structures created a lack of clarity as to with whom the actual power sat. When we left her, Nina was feeling uneasy about the security of her position on the team.

As Nina considered her options, she was met with her own personal crisis when her partner passed away after a short illness, rocking Nina to the core. Her partner had been otherwise young and healthy, so the grief was compounded by shock. Nina notified HR and was given a week of bereavement leave and told not to worry about a thing. Nina was a very private person and didn't talk much about her personal life at work, so she didn't tell anyone else what was going on. She had been around long enough at PArts to know how these things were handled. A respectfully worded message would be sent saying that Nina was experiencing a great personal loss and people should know she was out and should be gentle with her upon her return.

When she returned a week later, she was met with a pile of work and the general sense that she was behind. She was still grieving the sudden loss of her partner—no one can put a time limit on that kind of grief, but she didn't have any more leave time to take. And even if she did, she knew the work would just continue piling up. Yet her grief was intense and came in waves at the most unsuspecting moments. Even more surprising, it seemed no one had been told why she had been out. She was greeted with a variety of cordial "nice to have you back!" greetings when she joined meetings, but no one acknowledged any kind of loss. Nina was dumbfounded. This was not how things were done at PArts; why was this happening to her? She didn't have the emotional bandwidth to tell people or correct any misunderstanding, so she put her head down and tried, as best she could, to catch up with the work.

Two weeks following her bereavement leave, Jade scheduled a meeting with her. They were preparing for the upcoming all-hands. Jade was planning to do a full presentation from the perspective of her new role and would be presenting content from the AEC. She was also about to leave for a 10-day vacation. On the Friday before she left, Jade shared with Nina her plan for the meeting and asked her to schedule meetings with a variety of folks and do other preparatory tasks so things would continue to move along while she was out.

Nina was once again speechless. Jade's sense of superiority was infuriating. They had been equal partners in the AEC. Now she was treating Nina like her administrative assistant, asking her to prepare things for her while she was out on vacation. Not only that, Nina's partner had just died and she was still trying to get her bearings. All of this after Nina had willingly stepped in to support Jade for months of her own grieving process.

At the same time, Nina's relationship with Simone was becoming increasingly uncomfortable. With the backdrop of Simone becoming the new executive director and the knowledge that she didn't think Nina deserved her promotion, an ever-present tension colored their interactions, which were littered with many odd moments. Nina's effect was naturally "flat." She wasn't a highly emotive communicator, which was well known by anyone who worked with her. Simone once awkwardly called her out on it in front of others by saying, "Well, Nina's living over there in sarcasm-ville." Another time, in a small group setting, Simone had asked the group if there were any questions. When Nina asked a question, Simone paused, then asked if there were any *other* questions. Nina had no idea what to make of that.

As those types of moments stacked up, Simone scheduled an update meeting about a marketing project Nina was leading. She included the current executive director (as Simone herself had not yet taken over), Nina, and Jade. Nina couldn't understand why Jade was there, since she didn't play a role in this project. As the meeting went on, Nina grew increasingly uncomfortable with the tone of the meeting. Feeling like she was being grilled, she finally named her discomfort. She said that it felt as if she was being micromanaged and she didn't understand what they were trying to accomplish.

Simone ended the meeting abruptly, only to schedule a follow-up meeting with Nina and share that she had some feedback for her. She said she seemed to be out of sorts and Simone didn't appreciate how she was showing up with her colleagues. Nina's control of her emotions finally broke during this meeting. She said, "You know, my partner just passed away and I'm going through a lot." Simone claimed she did not know, which infuriated Nina. She couldn't believe the incoming leader of this organization wasn't aware of why she had suddenly been out for a week, but Simone held fast to her denial.

Then she shifted right back into delivering feedback. "When you ask the questions you ask, you undermine the entire organization." *What? How can one person undermine the organization with a single question?* Nina shared that, of course, it was not her intention to undermine anything with her questions; she was always simply seeking clarity. Simone responded, "Moving forward, when you speak in group settings or when you give feedback to your colleagues, I ask that you start by stating your purpose in the question you are about to ask so your intent is clear."

At this point, Nina had no idea how she would ever dig herself out of this hole. Why was she being asked to show up in a certain way? A way that was different from others? Why was her tone being policed? Why was she being asked to check her effect in conversions, when her effect was simply a part of her personality? Could she not be herself and do good work? It was then that she noticed none of the feedback being given was about her work product, her project leadership, or the skills for which she was hired.

Once regular "check-in" meetings with HR were scheduled, Nina knew she was being managed out. And she wouldn't give them the satisfaction. She had been thinking about starting her own digital marketing business, and this was the final nudge she needed to get that process going, and quickly.

Faith Is Lonely at the Edge of the Cliff

In Chapter 8, we saw Faith face the changing tide of public opinion. She saw nearly unanimous support as she took on the interim superintendent role and then immediately saw people turn against her when she started making changes that impacted them. The board was turned off by her honesty and her inability to just "make the problems go away," and the leadership team prioritized their own interests over the needs of the district as a whole.

Faith brought in an outside facilitator for the approaching leadership retreat. She wanted to be able to sit back and watch the dynamics unfold—this would be a true test of whether the team could come together and do what was right.

The facilitator laid out the problem at hand and set the team up for a working session to brainstorm solutions. There were some glimmers of hope—some conversations that seemed to be leaning toward banding together to make the tough call. But at the end of the day, the team came out divided, and the rationale for each person's position was clearly grounded in their own self-interest, not what was best for the organization. This team was not ready to come together for the good of the organization, and Faith realized then that her reputation was at stake if she was going to continue.

At that moment, Faith considered the possibility that she would reject the board's impending offer to stay on as permanent superintendent. But it was more than just a job for Faith. She was a young Black female educational leader, one of few across the entire country, let alone the state. She knew eyes would be on her, and she carried more than her own success on her shoulders. More than the success of the district, she also carried, albeit unfairly, the success of Black women leaders at the senior-most level in public education. If she failed at this job, she felt she would be failing on behalf of the entire group.

She didn't want to believe she could fail, but her first few months had indicated she certainly wasn't being set up to succeed. She was a strong leader. She knew she had it in her to carry the vision of the district forward. But she also knew that no individual person could do this alone. And her experience was falling right in line with a textbook example of the "glass cliff."

Shortly after the leadership retreat, the board began to put together the offer for the permanent position. Given Faith's history with the district, she had a relatively casual relationship with the board chair, so he approached the negotiations informally. He emailed a draft offer and she sent it to her lawyer for review. After discussing the terms, they felt disappointed. The salary was not competitive, not much more than she had accepted for the interim position and significantly less than her immediate predecessor had been offered. (More specifically, the offer was significantly less than earned by the male superintendent who had abandoned the role after just a few months.)

When Faith's attorney sent a response to the offer, the board chair was taken aback. He called Faith on her cell phone and started the conversation with, "Why are you getting your attorney involved?" No "Hello." Just an attack. Faith simply stated this was standard practice for superintendent contracts and directed him to continue communicating with her attorney. He was angry and offended, despite being a highly successful businessman who Faith was certain had attorneys negotiating on his behalf every day.

After a few weeks of arguing about whether or not her attorney was needed, Faith lost patience and broke the news to the board. She would not be continuing to negotiate and would be stepping down from the interim role. The health of the organization overall—her trust in the leadership team, her trust in the board to have her back when times were tough—wasn't enough to give her the confidence that she was being set up for success.

If Faith had thought the board behavior was unprofessional before, it became more so from this point on. Two of the board members started texting Faith during early morning hours asking to talk. They would have nothing of substance to talk about; their only aim was to get her to reconsider the offer. They said things like, "How can you walk away from this? Doesn't the district mean anything to you? It's a huge salary. Where else are you going to make that kind of money? I can't believe you are saying no." Their inability to take Faith seriously became increasingly evident by the day.

Once it was clear she wasn't going to change her mind, the two board members shifted their tactics. While they had been begging her to take the role, telling her she was the best person for it, they now started making comments to stakeholders about how she wasn't ready for the position. They said she wasn't strategic enough and openly suggested that she couldn't handle being a mother and holding this position.

The loneliness at the edge of the glass cliff was astounding. Faith had never felt more alone. Her longtime mentor and friend had led her blindly into a complete mess, her team didn't support her vision and direction, and the board seemed to be prepared to push her right over the edge if she had stayed. Faith kept her head held high and stood firm on her reason for leaving. As the board continued to put energy into crafting their own narrative regarding her departure, they failed to move quickly (or seemingly at all) to take action on what would happen next. Faith had to continually remind them that she was leaving on June 30, whether they found a replacement or not. Even in her departure, Faith was being set up to take the blame for their lack of action.

 Consider taking a moment in the companion journal to reflect on each of our friends' "rock bottom" moment.

PART IV

Finding Inspiration

"You will burn and you will burn out; you will be healed and come back again."

— Fyodor Dostoevsky

Chapter 11
Our Friends Find a Path Forward

In the previous chapter, we saw our friends hit rock bottom. In each and every case, they realized significant change was necessary to preserve their own physical, mental, and emotional health.

In this chapter, we will see the beginnings of Dostoevsky's promise to our friends: "You will be healed, and come back again." We see our friends putting their own needs above the needs of others. We see them setting boundaries and surrounding themselves with people who build them up rather than tear them down.

In this section, we break from our established pattern and go directly to our friends' stories to first learn how they each resolved their situations. Then, in Chapter 12, we will use inspiration from our friends to speak generally to the idea of finding a path forward.

As we follow our friends to the end of this book, let's consider how the end of each story represents the beginning of something better—how each of our friends recognized that, in the words of Paulo Coelho, they "deserve the love and care [they] give to others."

"My health matters." ~ Miah

With the extra week of short-term disability, Miah considered a plan for a more immediate change. When she took the manager role, she knew it would be time-bound due to the long commute, and she had about a year left on that clock. All this time, she felt responsible for sticking it out for that predetermined amount of time. She loved her team, and she was proud of the work they had done to build the program. Yet, the last year had taken a major toll on Miah.

As Miah considered her options, she noticed something about the people around her. For starters, her husband had left his job the previous June. It was a job he thought was going to be his life's work, but when the job started taking an ever-increasing emotional and physical toll on him, he decided to leave. Miah witnessed the positive impact of that transition every day.

Miah also had a friend who left a job during the time she was on medical leave. This friend turned her back on a toxic work environment, and Miah herself had encouraged and supported her along the way. Seeing how just making the decision to leave had impacted this friend, suddenly Miah's next move was clear.

She would find a way to return the following week and would give her two weeks' notice. It was going to be hard, but Miah knew that she had the support system to do it. With an end in sight, she thought she would be able to make it back and see it through. It wasn't going to be an easy two weeks, but she could do it. Even if she needed to get a ride, Miah was finally going to put her health first.

The next Monday, Miah scheduled a meeting with Andie and handed in her resignation letter. Andie was furious, but she had no choice but to accept it. Miah spent the rest of the week notifying her team and other colleagues and, with support from her husband and friends, was able to manage their various responses. Miah held firm to the decision being about her health and deflected all the anger and sadness her colleagues projected. Colleagues who truly cared about Miah were supportive, of course.

Miah knew it would take time to fully recover—both physically and emotionally, but she was finally on a path to freedom. Miah knew that whatever her next step was, it would be one that prioritized treating people with compassion and respect and brought people together rather than drove them apart.

"I refuse to change." ~ Briana

Looking in the mirror and asking through flowing tears, "Who am I?" was the moment Briana recognized how much this job was changing her. And she couldn't let that happen. She had to get out before permanent damage was done. Deep down, she knew she was a confident, competent contributor, and she wouldn't let anyone else tell her otherwise.

Briana wiped her eyes, took a deep breath, and endured the rest of the day knowing she was going to make a plan to get out.

That night, Briana talked to her husband who was more than supportive of the decision. They spent a week preparing her resume for job hunting, but agreed she shouldn't wait to give her notice. She had to start the clock on her departure before it was too late.

The following Monday, Briana gave her two weeks' notice. Linda was shocked and asked her to please consider giving a longer window for transition. Briana said she would consider it, but the next day let her know she would be leaving in two weeks. Her experience had told her there were no boundaries at this workplace and there was no urgency to fill a vacancy when safety nets were available. How long had she supported Karen while they were supposedly searching for a new administrative assistant? And if Briana had to be on call at all times during a company-wide shutdown, how could she expect to be treated after giving notice when there was nothing to lose by treating her poorly?

The next two weeks were awkward at best. A few times a week, Linda dropped passive aggressive one-liners about being left in a lurch and not having any good help around here. Briana survived each day by reminding herself that it was almost over.

While she didn't have a job lined up by her last day, she did have interviews scheduled and was optimistic about the prospects. And she knew as she headed into those interviews to trust her instincts. If she ever again got a weird feeling about a potential boss in an interview, she would lean into those feelings and ask more questions.

"There is more than one way to do good in the world." ~ Evelyn

A week after the trip to Africa, Evelyn was finally well enough to return to the office and tender her resignation. She was disappointed to leave a place doing such good work, but she just couldn't live with the double standard that was the Rise Foundation. To be so committed to advocating for women's rights and to treat the women who work for you so poorly, it just didn't make any sense to Evelyn.

Evelyn had been committed to working in nonprofit organizations with the thought that these organizations would be the best way to do good in the world. After leaving Rise, she subsequently landed in two other places that were plagued with different versions of toxic work culture. Ultimately, this led to Evelyn becoming completely disenfranchised with the idea of nonprofit work.

The next place Evelyn worked at seemed great at first, until she noticed the board of directors getting involved in the daily management of the work. She was hired for her expertise given her involvement with Rise, but her opinion was often overruled by the desires of board members. When the executive director left, the spouse of a board member was named interim without any transparent process, which certainly raised some eyebrows. There were additional issues with nepotism, including a cover-up of an abuse allegation directed at a staff member whose parent was on the board.

Evelyn's third place of employment was more of the same: long hours, no boundaries, and unprofessional commentary from the boss regarding what Evelyn wore and how she looked. Add that into the low pay, part-time hours, and "above and beyond" expectations. The part-time hours, however, allowed Evelyn to start building a freelance graphic design business, but the lack of boundaries and over-the-top expectations created roadblocks.

Again, Evelyn's expertise was overlooked, and she wasn't able to contribute in ways she knew she could. Evelyn had not even been working for 10 years and was already jaded—she couldn't help but wonder whether this was how it would be in every nonprofit organization.

Finally, Evelyn needed a break. She was a talented designer and she knew that if she committed to it, she could make a living doing freelance graphic design. Would that alone make a difference? Making logos and websites? Designing marketing materials? Probably not, but Evelyn also realized that how you make a living is not the only way to do good in the world. If she could make ends meet (or better) with her design work, she would have the time and the resources to contribute in other ways—volunteering, making donations, and otherwise getting involved in her community.

This mindset shift allowed Evelyn to see the value in her skills and what she had to offer, and she was able to feel comfortable with her contribution to the causes she cared about. She could make a difference in a different way.

"I refuse to be treated as 'less than.'" ~ Nina

As soon as Nina received the formal incorporation papers for her business, she gave her resignation notice to PArts. She wanted to keep her integrity intact and leave on good terms, so she followed the most professional approach. Since she had no manager of record, Nina sent her resignation letter to HR and to Simone, as the incoming executive director. She gave four weeks' notice and waited for a response before telling anyone else.

And she waited. And waited. And waited.

Nina received no response from either HR or Simone. No acknowledgement, no offer to have a conversation. For more than two weeks, she worked with the knowledge that she would be leaving the organization without anyone else being aware. Finally, just more than a week before her last day, she got a response. It said, "Please talk to anyone you would like to inform personally of your departure today. We are going to announce it at the full team meeting this afternoon."

That's it. No, "Thanks for the three years of work at this organization." No, "Will that be enough time for you to talk to people individually?" No, "We're sorry to see you leave."

Ultimately, this response underscored her decision. Nina felt completely dehumanized. She had behaved in a way that valued the humanity of her colleagues, even when it took a tremendous toll on her, but that humanity was not reciprocated. Her personal crisis was ignored while someone else's was treated with the utmost care and respect. Her promotion and recognition was kept under wraps while others were celebrated. And now, her resignation was being treated as a formality, not as a teammate leaving after more than three years.

Simone did request one final meeting with Nina before she left, primarily to hand off some of the work. Simone shared a striking reflection in that meeting. She said, "I feel like now that you are leaving I can talk to you like a human." Nina didn't respond, but she would have liked to say, "I've been a human the whole time. Perhaps if you had talked to me like a human, we wouldn't be here right now."

The broader team was shocked to learn of Nina's departure. She couldn't even begin to explain her reasons to all of the people who reached out with concern. She never said it out loud, but the simplest answer was also the most obvious. When you lose someone close to you and can't get an ounce of support from your organization, of course you are going to leave. But still, no one was aware of what she had gone through.

Nina walked away quietly and spent the better portion of the next year healing and building her business before she even considered joining another organization. She knows now more than ever that her humanity matters too.

"My daughter is watching." ~ Faith

At long last, the board signed a contract with an experienced interim superintendent and planned for a two-month transition period. Faith finally felt herself being pulled back from the edge of the cliff.

The new interim started on May 1, and the laborious two-month transition period began. Faith's experience over that time period underscored her decision to walk away. Her main reason for leaving had been the lack of support from the board, the team, and the general public.

It was frustrating to see the board's response to the new interim, who happened to have a different racial identity than Faith. Challenges she had brought up before that had been dismissed by the board were suddenly heard and validated, and the new interim was offered support when concerns were noted.

Perhaps they had finally learned their lesson, but Faith couldn't help but wonder what could have been had they offered her that same support.

Faith saw situations continue where her voice was not valued, despite all her experience. She was almost entirely dismissed by the board in deference to the new interim, who didn't have the benefit of Faith's years of experience with the district.

Faith knew her decision was the right one, and she walked away with her head held high. Integrity always was and continues to be the most important personal value to Faith. She would never engage in work she didn't believe in or couldn't fully support. She would always remain true to her values and would only align herself with people who shared them.

Now that Faith was a mom, she lived her life according to one dominant guiding principle:

> *My daughter is watching. She will see how I behave. She will see how I let others treat me. If the schools I'm in charge of aren't good enough for her, and if people around me aren't committed to doing what is necessary to make them so, I won't have any part of it.*
>
> *My daughter is watching.*

 Head over to the companion journal to reflect on the ways in which our friends found peace and resolution in their unique challenges.

Chapter 12

Finding Your Path

Working for a mission-driven organization should be life-giving—*and it can completely drain the life out of you.*

You can love the work you are meant to do—*and hate your job.*

You can care about the kids (or clients, or patients)—*at the expense of caring for yourself.*

Mission-driven work is good work. So many problems exist in the world, and without these organizations and the people who believe that change is possible, we would never make any progress. People who are drawn to mission-driven work care about the mission. They can and do love to work for a cause. They love knowing their work contributes to a greater good. Whether their work is client-facing or not, they care about the kids, the patients, the people on the other end of the work.

All of this can be true *and* your work can drain the life out of you. The work is good *and* the workplace not so much. You end up prioritizing the mission over yourself. You try to meet the expectations of an unrealistic or narcissistic boss. You get constantly undermined by your colleagues. You get reminded constantly of your mistakes, even when you have owned and corrected them. Your health suffers. Your relationships suffer. Your work takes over your life. If you could just work a little harder, get through this hump, have one win… it will all be worth it.

In this book, we have followed our friends through their own destructive journeys, and we have come out with them on the other side. We've seen them walk this path—starting out with the bright-eyed optimism this work provides. We've seen them shell-shocked by the reality awaiting them and the confusion when their colleagues' actions and behaviors did not match the goodness of the mission.

And we've seen them emerge from the depths of their demoralization, from illness and emptiness, inspired to take a step into a brighter reality and a return to optimism. Our friends were able to turn things around. And you can too.

Escaping toxic environments does not mean you have to give up on your passion. What it does mean is you are willing to show yourself you deserve to be whole and human at work. Organizations exist that do good work and have a positive work environment. And if enough people start to speak up about and call out toxic work culture, the organizations that fall short will be forced to change.

Your job is not a life sentence, no matter how much good it has the potential to do.

Our Friends' Experiences: The Punchline

Miah recognized how the last year had taken a toll on her health. Through her medical leave, she had a glimpse of what freedom from this job could look like. And she knew she couldn't stand by and watch all of her hard work from the years prior continue to be torn apart by her boss. She took the brave step to resign and focus on her family and her health.

Briana got fed up with the constant reminders of past mistakes. She got tired of walking on eggshells and making more mistakes than she normally would have because of her fear and anxiety about making them. She recognized as she cried in the bathroom that this job was breaking her. And she decided at that moment to leave.

Evelyn started her nonprofit career in an organization dedicated to empowering and uplifting women—just not the women who worked at the organization. Evelyn was poorly compensated, treated unprofessionally, and expected to "get over it" and "be grateful" whenever she suffered. She then experienced various flavors of toxicity in her next two nonprofit jobs as well. Finally, Evelyn decided that working for a nonprofit wasn't the only way to make a difference in the world. She could tap into her talent for graphic design and start her own business, all while having time and energy to volunteer and contribute to her community in other ways.

Nina was baffled by the double standard she was experiencing at her organization. She saw the way other people were treated, and she couldn't figure out why she wasn't being given the same courtesy and compassion. She saw the writing on the wall and decided then and there she had to go. Knowing she needed to set herself up before she left, she started working on building a consulting business. As soon as Nina was in a position where she felt comfortable making a move, she followed through.

Faith discovered she wasn't ever going to be successful in her role leading such a dysfunctional organization. She saw how everyone who had supported her placement in the role was putting up barriers and roadblocks at every turn and how many of those same people were turning against her. She saw the toll it was going to take on her personally, but also recognized the significance of her position. She was not prepared to be the next example of a Black woman put in a position of leadership and set up to fail.

Our friends got out of their toxic environments. And it was hard. They cared about the mission, they saw how the organizations they worked in were poised to do good work. Yet they chose to leave. Some endured negativity and judgment or feelings of guilt as they exited. But they did it because they deserved better.

We all deserve better. We deserve to work in a place that treats us well, one that supports us in times of need, that builds us up rather than breaks us down, that cares about us as humans *in addition to* caring about the people we serve. The mission matters, but the people doing the work matter too.

Clarity and Validation

After I decided to leave a job that was not good for me, I began talking to people about it. And that's when I started seeing it everywhere. I soon realized that not only was I not the problem, I was also not the only one experiencing this.

This book exists because I believe that, sometimes, all it takes is watching someone else go through a challenging event to see things more clearly for ourselves.

- Miah watched both her husband and her friend suffer from toxic environments and then choose to leave. She saw the similarities in her own experience and found the strength to make a change.

- Briana watched how colleagues at her organization were treated and combined that with her own experience to catalyze her change.

Perhaps you have "watched" Miah, Briana, Evelyn, Nina, and Faith go through their own challenging events and it gave you some clarity about what you or someone you love is experiencing. Perhaps you've wondered whether it was somehow your fault, and now you see that it was not. Perhaps you've wondered whether this was how it had to be, and now you see that it didn't have to be this way. Perhaps you've wondered whether you were being selfish for feeling like you didn't want to keep toiling away "for the mission," and now you see that you matter more.

Now What?

If you feel validated by what you have read in this book, then it has done what it was supposed to do. I want readers to see they are not alone and the experiences they are having don't have to be tolerated. But clarity alone doesn't help with much until we take action. So you might be asking—what can I do about it? Is leaving the only option? Or maybe you are thinking, "I can't leave; now is not the right time."

Yes, all of our friends found their path forward by leaving the jobs that were failing them. But that doesn't mean it's the only option. To be clear—it *might* be the best option. But you can take some steps before getting to that place, especially if leaving is going to be a challenge financially. Only you will know what options are right for you.

My intent here is to lay out some considerations. I recommend working with a trusted friend or advisor to navigate your particular situation.

Get Perspective

Sometimes we are so caught up in our daily experiences, it's hard to see what is actually happening. So, before jumping into any next steps, be sure your perspective is clear. Mentors and a supportive network (more on these later in this chapter) can be helpful with this step, especially in providing objectivity with respect to what is going on. Gary Chapman identifies two main components to gaining perspective:

- **See through the fog**: Oftentimes difficult work environments are complex. You have one lens into what is happening, but there might be many factors of which you are unaware. "Seek clarity about what's really going on, consult with your bases of support, and take carefully considered action."

- **Compare best practices**: You might have someone telling you that what you're experiencing is "just how it is" with this kind of work. And if you are new to the workforce, you likely won't have anything to compare it to. Trust your gut if you think something is off. Talk to other people to build a picture of what is going on in other organizations. [22]

Once you have a fuller perspective and some validation for what you are seeing as the problem, you are ready to take some action.

Catalyze a Shift in Culture

Depending on the extent of the toxic culture in your organization, you will first want to consider whether or not there is an opportunity to incite change for the better. Is the culture problem widespread? Is it contained to a single team? Are others facing this problem or is it just you?

If it feels manageable (never easy, but *manageable*), you might put some effort into trying to contribute to the betterment of the organization. Included among a number of ways this could be tackled are:

- Give direct feedback to the individual at the heart of the issue.

- Gather a group of people having a common experience and band together to effect change across the organization.

- Raise a concern to human resources or a person in a position of authority who can bring the need for change to leadership.

None of this will be easy, of course, but it's always best to consider whether you can turn a challenge into an opportunity for growth—because if the culture can be fixed, then you might be able to prioritize yourself and the mission without sacrificing either.

Protect Yourself

If you are experiencing toxic leadership in the form of narcissistic abuse (in particular, the gaslighting and DIMMER behaviors discussed in Chapter 3) and you need to stay in your role for the time being, Dr. Durvasula recommends a few tactics that can help you to protect yourself.

- **Set boundaries**: As we discussed earlier, boundaries are impossible without the structural support to uphold them. In a healthy work culture, boundaries are about collective accountability. With an abusive boss, boundaries have to be viewed as one-sided. It's an opportunity for you to think clearly about what you will and won't tolerate and to be prepared to say no when the boundary is crossed. Realistically, you can't expect the abuser to respect the boundaries, so you have to be ready to say no and stick to it.

- **Minimize contact**: This is a tough one if the toxic relationship is your boss, but one way to minimize the impact of a difficult relationship is to reduce your contact with that person. Some strategies might include only opening emails and other communication from this person at a predetermined time of the week, or limiting your face-to-face interactions by physically moving the location of your desk in the office.

- **Find your true north**: This recommendation is a little bit like the common parenting advice of "pick your battles." In toxic relationships, you have control over how you choose to engage. If you spend time thinking about what matters most to you in the relationship, you can choose to let things go when they are about something that is not your "true north."

- **Don't go DEEP (Defend, Explain, Engage, or Personalize)**: If you have experience dealing with a narcissistic person, you know that these behaviors are ones that send you down a rabbit hole of self-doubt and self-blame. You can't win an argument with a narcissist—so don't try. Avoid defensiveness. Keep your engagement as transactional as possible. If you are far enough into a relationship with a narcissistic person, you know that they are not going to change. You have to start practicing radical acceptance and expecting them to behave in this way, even when they might show a glimmer of hope of changing. Expecting more will only lead to disappointment.

Toxic managers can do a lot of damage to a person's psyche and their emotional and physical health. While I have provided some suggestions of how to manage this relationship, these dynamics are incredibly complicated. If you are struggling with a manager or a colleague who is displaying narcissistic tendencies, seek professional support. The book I have referenced here, *It's Not You: Identifying and Healing from Narcissistic People* by Ramani Durvasula, PhD, is a good place to start.

Get Support

It is worth noting that none of our friends actively sought professional mental health services during our glimpse into their stories. The ones who experienced physical symptoms did seek medical attention, but there was no explicit mention of mental health services. It is also worth noting that employer-supported medical leave is primarily focused on the treatment of physical conditions—or it is at least more socially acceptable to take a leave for physical conditions.

Times are changing in this respect, with a lot of companies increasing support for mental health and providing better mental health benefits. Look into your company's health benefits and see what's available. A mental health professional can be an incredible asset for navigating challenging professional relationships.

Whatever you do, don't navigate a toxic work environment alone. This is where you start to question your own perception of things. "Is it me?" You need people to build you up when the people around you are breaking you down.

If your organization is large and you trust some of your colleagues, you might be able to build a supportive internal network. Those people will understand your context and are likely as committed to the mission as you are. As Chapman, White, and Myra note, "Even in dysfunctional cultures, good relationships can be nurtured." [23]

Of course, the risk of attempting to build a community of support within your organization is twofold. One, you need to be sure your level of trust is high and that your colleagues won't undermine you. Two, you need to be cautious of this network devolving into a gossip session that contributes to the toxic culture of the workplace rather than working to fix it or even just helping you navigate it.

A far less risky option is to lean on an external network of support. Having a group of trusted advisors, whether they are friends, family, or former colleagues, can provide you with the much needed perspective and be an extremely safe space to work through the situations you are facing. I have been leading professional cohorts of women who come together for learning and mutual support and have seen this kind of structure be incredibly effective—especially if you don't have an established network at the ready.

In addition, research supports the value of mentorship in professional development. Specifically, research shows that "people who identify mentors and then nurture those relationships are the ones who most often succeed in life and work. Wise mentors supply many advantages including objectivity—vital for surviving toxic cultures." [24]

Consider a Change in Role

Depending on the size of your organization and the kind of work you do, an internal shift might be enough to remove you from the toxic situation. If your toxic situation primarily stems from the team you are on, could there be a way to contribute your skills and expertise on a new team? If it's related to your immediate supervisor, is there a way to change the reporting structure? Or, if your organization has different geographic locations, do your current life circumstances give you the flexibility to request a transfer?

Develop an Exit Plan

Even if you ultimately decide you must leave, you don't have to give notice tomorrow.

If you have considered (or even done) the things listed above and have seen no improvement, you might just need to start developing an exit strategy. Again, you don't need to give your notice tomorrow, but sit down with a supportive family member, a friend, a mentor, or a therapist and make a plan. How can you carve out time to start searching for jobs? Build your network? Can you start to put money away in savings to cover you for a period of unemployment?

But most of all—set a target date. Give yourself a date by which you will resign. Don't get stuck in the trap of always kicking it out to a later date because "it's not the right time." I've seen people stay in jobs for years because of this cycle. Things get bad, they decide they need to leave. Things get better and they think, "I can manage this." Then things inevitably get bad again, and the cycle continues.

This is not to say that you should quit a job the moment anything gets hard. That's not what we are talking about here; rather, our discussion is focused on a pervasive toxic culture that you have genuinely tried to address and have been unsuccessful. This is a culture that is affecting your physical and mental health, a culture that has extinguished the passion you had for the work at the outset.

The Role Work Plays in Our Lives

Another question to ask yourself is how much space does work take up in your life? How much of your time and energy is devoted to it? Where else do you put time and energy?

Leaving mission-driven work can be hard as a result of the space it can take up in our lives. Often, we are so committed to the mission that it can be all-consuming. This is great—until it isn't.

When we lose ourselves to the work, our identity becomes tied to it. We don't have energy to dedicate to other things—family, friends, community, hobbies, interests, etc. As a result, when and if we consider leaving a job, it feels as though we are effectively leaving ourselves. "If I don't do this, who am I?"

In his book, *The Good Enough Job*, Simone Stolzoff challenges the notion that the only way to fulfillment is through finding work that incorporates your passion. Sure, the old adage of "do what you love and never work a day in your life" can be true for some, but it's not the only path. Work can be a means to an end: it can give you the resources you need to pursue your passion elsewhere, or do what you love in your time outside of work. And Stolzoff argues that no matter what our jobs are, we need to diversify our identity by spending time and energy on things outside of work.

One particular recommendation is to take time to define what a healthy relationship with work means to you. What role do you want work to play? What other aspects of your life are important to you? What indicators will be on your radar that might signify your relationship with work is no longer healthy? As Stolzoff wisely notes, "If you don't take the time to define it for yourself, your employer will gladly do it for you." [25]

Final Thoughts

In the words of Russian novelist Fyodor Dostoevsky, "You will burn and you will burn out; you will be healed and come back again." Even if you have hit rock bottom, there is hope.

If anything you read in this book resonates with your experience, know that you are not alone. Know that you deserve better. You deserve a workplace that not only supports its mission, but also supports the people doing the work. If you are not being supported in the way you need in order to be your best self, you will feel the impact, and it's not worth it.

See it for what it is and what it isn't: it's not you.

Find your people. Build your support systems. Prioritize yourself.

And when you are ready, make the change you need to make.

Reclaim your passion. It's not selfish. If you've been let down, now is the time to rise up and heal from the broken promises.

 Find space in the companion journal to reflect on how these suggestions resonate and can be applied to your own situation. Don't forget to head back here to read the Author's Note and the Epilogue.

 Author's Note

*Understanding the Toxic Workplace
In Female-Dominated Industries*

I would be remiss if I didn't acknowledge the prominence of women in these stories.

Mission-driven work is female dominated. Teaching, nursing, community development, social work, etc. The data is clear—there are more women in these industries than there are men.

I intentionally chose to profile the stories of women. My work centers around the experiences of women in the workplace, and while it is not only women who experience toxic culture, it felt important to me to highlight the experiences of women.

You may have also noticed that women were also the primary antagonists in most of the stories you read. So, yes, these are cases where women are causing emotional harm to other women. Women are not exempt from toxic behaviors by nature of our gender. So much of what we have internalized as acceptable behavior has been communicated through the same societal experiences as our male counterparts, based in patriarchy, racism, and sexism.

Gender is an important consideration in discussing these issues. Individual identities do play a role in how relationships are navigated. And claiming a particular identity does not "give you a pass" from having to reflect critically on how you are behaving in the workplace and the world.

Please do not misunderstand the story that is being told here. Mission-driven workplaces are not toxic because they are female dominated. Mission-driven workplaces breed toxicity for all of the reasons discussed in this book.

I believe in navigating the world with clear principles and values, and I believe there is nuance to almost every situation. I hope this book has provided some food for thought in this regard.

Epilogue

"Courage is more exhilarating than fear and in the long run it is easier. We do not have to become heroes overnight. Just a step at time, meeting each thing that comes up, seeing it is not as dreadful as it appeared, discovering we have the strength to stare it down."

— Eleanor Roosevelt

♋ Advice From Our Friends

Dear Reader,

Please join me in sharing tremendous gratitude to the five women who bravely shared their stories with me for inclusion in this book. Without them, the purpose of this book—validation, comfort, inspiration, and learning—would not have been possible.

While these are real women and their stories are true, as noted, names and identifying details including industry, geography, and other elements of setting have been changed to protect their anonymity.

These brave women shared their stories with me in a single interview. Once the book was written, I asked each to read my interpretation to ensure the essence of her experience remained intact. At that point, I invited our friends to share a message directly with you, to give a sense of their lessons learned and where they are now.

Included here are messages from our friends directly to you.

Letter From Miah

Dear Reader,

My experience nearly destroyed my love for the work, the very topic, and my colleagues. I continue to be grateful for my decision to leave, and I am recovering, though slowly. Were it not for the last 18 months in this role, I would not have made several subsequent big (and brave) decisions that have set my life on a completely new course. So even though it's now almost a year after my last day, I still struggle to hear the ongoing news of what happened to my program and my colleagues—the patient outcomes are devastating to me, but I am learning that taking care of myself matters.

I think many of us who choose mission-driven work are at risk of completely wearing ourselves out in service of others, a dangerous habit in the context of profit-driven systems. The impact on our souls and bodies is rarely considered; we will, after all, just be replaced by the next body and soul. I waited too long to leave, believing everything would stop for me if I did. And partly, that is true. I stopped rushing—in the car, for sure, but also in everyday tasks. I am working on being fully present when I'm in conversation with someone I love—precious time I also rushed before. By the time I got home, I realized I gave the best of me to other people and didn't have much left for my partner, and our daughter, not to mention my friends. Recently, I spent a week with an old friend who shared with me she felt she "had me back" after a long absence, that I was myself again.

I do not know if I will seek another role like this; I need more time to prepare myself. I know this, because the role I accepted after I left—a remote part-time teaching job for a program I was only somewhat familiar with but believed I knew enough about the program director to feel it was a supportive environment—proved to be oddly similar to what I had left. This time, though, I knew exactly when it was time to walk away and not renew the contract. And my life is not just about work now—it's about living my values as fully as possible, which includes honoring my voice and my health.

About 10 months after it appeared, my vertigo is now gone, and my heart continues to heal.

To healing,

Miah

Letter From Briana

Dear Reader,

By now you've read the story of my personal experience working with a boss whose leadership style was toxic, overbearing, and ultimately detrimental to my professional and personal well-being. My hope is that others can learn from my experience and recognize the signs of a harmful work environment before it affects their mental health and productivity.

Now that I'm safely on the other side of this experience I am grateful for the opportunity to share directly with you. When I worked at the "Great Lakes Regional Youth Development Organization," I found myself working for a manager who, at first glance, seemed driven and passionate. However, it soon became clear that their leadership style was more about control than empowerment. This individual would micromanage every aspect of the team's work, from minute details to long-term projects. There was no room for creativity or independent thought, and little room for any mistakes. Every task was subject to their approval, often resulting in unnecessary delays and stress.

Beyond the constant micromanagement, the work environment became increasingly toxic. Feedback was rarely constructive; instead, it was often laced with criticism and negativity. This created an atmosphere of fear and led to a breakdown in communication and collaboration within the team. I saw colleagues, once motivated and eager to contribute, become anxious and disengaged.

Perhaps the most difficult aspect of working under such a manager was the lack of respect for personal boundaries. Long hours became the norm, and there was an expectation to be constantly available, even during personal time. Any effort to set healthy work–life boundaries was met with frustration or reprimand, contributing to an overwhelming sense of burnout.

What I've learned from this experience is the importance of advocating for yourself in the workplace. Recognize the signs of a toxic work environment early: lack of trust, unrealistic expectations, and an overall atmosphere of fear or negativity. If you find yourself in this situation, it's crucial to communicate your concerns, either directly with the individual or through the appropriate channels in your organization.

Equally important is the realization that no job is worth sacrificing your mental health. If the situation does not improve, be willing to explore other opportunities where you can thrive in a supportive, empowering environment.

A healthy workplace is one that fosters collaboration, values its employees, and encourages growth—not one that drains your energy and creativity. To anyone who finds themselves in a similar situation, know that you're not alone and options are available to you. These options might not be easy to attain but are definitely worth exploring. No one should endure a toxic work environment, and advocating for yourself is the first step toward creating a healthier professional journey.

Despite the pain I endured, I am also grateful for the experience, as it has taught me the significance of staying true to myself and helped me clearly identify what genuine leadership looks like.

Stay true to yourself,

Letter From Evelyn

Dear Reader,

You hear stories about toxic culture, and you know it's a reality. But when you start working at a nonprofit, where the mission drives the work and the impact is making positive change in the world, you go into it not expecting to experience toxic culture. You think, "It's not going to happen here." So it feels worse. I think it feels especially defeating and crushing to go into a field where you already know you're not doing it for the money, and then not only are you underpaid but also treated badly. Acknowledging this reality can be heartbreaking.

Don't ignore that little voice inside you. If something feels icky, then you're not imagining it. Don't let it pass—whether it's having that meeting, naming an uncomfortable thing, finding an ally in the office, or getting a new job. My advice is to just do something. And if you have to leave, so be it. It's not a reflection on you for leaving mission-driven work. I think I probably stayed in a couple of these bad situations longer than I should have, because I cared so much.

And in a way, I think a lot of those jobs thrive on the fact that they are female-dominant industries. The people drawn to these jobs put other people's needs first. Then the leadership, whether they are aware of it or not, takes advantage of the fact that women are already used to putting themselves second.

I wouldn't necessarily say, "Don't work in the nonprofit or a mission-driven industry." But going in, be really aware that it might not be all that different. And know you can ask questions of your leadership. It's a two-way street. I wish I had known that and had spoken up in these situations. I don't know if it would have changed anything, but I wish I'd asked certain questions in hindsight.

In hopes that my story helps you seek what you deserve,

Evelyn

Letter From Nina

Dear Reader,

I write this short note somewhat removed from the experience you've just read—removed in time and space, but not unaffected. As I've taken strides toward a new future, the challenges of my experience have shaped my mindset, my boundaries, and my self-advocacy.

I advocate for myself now more than ever. I encourage you to do the same. The only people who benefit from our silence are those who abuse and dehumanize us.

And so I further encourage you to stay grounded in your inherent value and worth as a human being. The workplaces that seek to steal these very things from us are just that—workplaces. And the people who inhabit them only do so for a time. Like you and me, those who occupy positions of social and positional power are temporary fixtures in environments that aren't capable of determining their worth.

The moment these individuals close their laptops, or walk out the office doors, or leave the job entirely, they cease to have the power that allows them to cause harm in the first place. They are, after all, human. Perhaps they are disconnected from that fact, but you don't have to be.

There's so much power (and empowerment) in knowing you are in control of your own destiny, and no matter how much others try to derail you, you can set your course anew—in your own time and as you wish.

In gratitude,

Nina

Letter From Faith

Dear Reader,

In this book you learned a lot about my professional work history. From my earliest work experience with a toxic leader and how it influenced my own leadership journey, to what should have been the ultimate leadership moment—and seeing that crumble due to toxic culture.

I am happy to share that I am now a reformed workaholic. I am living proof you can do great work and yet have work not be your life. I am back in a leadership role at a nonprofit organization and still working through the lessons I learned from my time at "RPSD." I prioritize time with my daughter, I have spent time rebuilding relationships with my extended family, and I continue to hold my values front and center as I navigate workplace dynamics.

Every once in a while, I still think about what "could have been" had I been able to stay in my role at RPSD. At the end of the day, it wasn't the right environment for me, and I'm proud I had the strength to step down. My advice to you is to trust your gut. Don't just give up when things get hard, but keep your eyes wide open, and if you think you are being set up to fail, you probably are.

Please know you deserve to be in a place that values you and wants you to be successful.

Faith

⚮ Final Words From the Author

Dear Reader,

Thank you for taking the time to read *Promises Broken*.

The primary purpose of this book was not to share my own story, and I want to reiterate that my story is *not* one of the five stories represented in *Promises Broken*. That being said, my experience was certainly a motivating factor for me to write this. I described a scene in the Introduction in which I had allowed myself to become the victim of a toxic work environment. I take full responsibility for my decisions along the way, decisions which landed me in emergency surgery. For the eight months leading up to that moment, I knew I was in pain and I wasn't taking care of myself. And I knew I wasn't putting as much energy as I wanted into my personal relationships. But I continued to prioritize work to avoid the repercussions of falling further behind in a job that was already drowning me. My circumstances were such that I was able to easily put everything else on the back burner, but that doesn't mean that deprioritizing those things was right.

Sometimes our bodies simply take control. Mine did, and it told me to STOP. It had been trying to tell me more gently, but I didn't listen. My body finally lost its patience and gave me no other choice.

When I decided to resign after returning from medical leave, it felt like a weight had been lifted from my shoulders. I stayed in the role for an extended transition period, but knowing there was an end in sight allowed me to recognize and deal with the things that had been weighing me down before.

For the first few months after leaving the job, I was exhausted—physically, mentally, emotionally. I was filled with self-doubt. I often felt like a failure. I had a hard time remembering the 25-plus years of positive work experience that predated this one experience. I was worried about finances and getting back on track. And still, I knew the decision was right for me. Alongside the understandable sense of worry was an underlying calm.

During this time, I found a few resources that were incredibly helpful to me, and I want to share them with you.

First, I am a reader, and reading was cathartic in my healing process. In the pages that follow, I have listed the nonfiction books that helped me on this journey. I would be remiss if I didn't also acknowledge the role that reading fiction plays in my life. I read nearly 100 novels during my medical leave and into the year following my surgery. I allowed myself to lean into the lives of others, lose myself in a different context, and make connections with my own experiences—and my recovery would have been very different without that part of my life.

Connecting with people was something that provided support in countless ways. Two things really worked well for me:

- **Try something new.** I signed up for a virtual publishing conference when I thought I might write a book but wasn't fully committed. The connections and networking opportunities through that conference provided validation for not only my experience but also for the idea of the book. When enough people tell you "I would read that book," it helps you turn a difficult situation into something amazing.

- **Maintain supportive relationships.** I have a few friends and former coworkers who were incredibly supportive of me. (You know who you are!) Find your people and let them know how you are doing. On the other hand, do not hang on to relationships that drain you, make you question your worth, or validate the toxic messages you are trying to escape. Leave behind those who drag you down, and spend time with those who lift you up.

Over the last year, while writing this book, I reflected on the breadth of valuable experience in my career, took a leap of faith, and launched my own business. I founded Almavina Strategic Partners to catalyze strong and healthy mission-driven organizations who embrace, honor, and value leaders of all identities. In particular, we focus our work on people and systems—developing communities of emerging female leaders, supporting women to build a strong and healthy presence in the workplace, and providing frameworks, tools, and strategies to support overall organizational health.

If you are looking for a place to find a mentor or a supportive community of professional women to help you navigate a transition, overcome workplace challenges, and break down barriers, or if you just want to share your own personal story and be heard, please visit us at www.almavina.com or connect with us on Instagram (@almavinareads) or LinkedIn (@beth-cocuzza). We'd love to hear from you!

Wishing you peace and productivity, rest and renewal, today, tomorrow, and always,

Beth

Join our community! If you are not yet a subscriber to our newsletter, please sign up today at www.almavina.com/signup.

Did this book have a positive impact on you and/or the way you view mission-driven work culture? If you purchased this book online and are so inclined, a positive review would be most appreciated. Help me spread the word!

Notes & References

Endnotes

Chapter 3

1. "Townhouse Notes: Toxic Work Environments: The History of an Idea | Perspectives on History | AHA."
2. "Toxic Workplace," Wikipedia.
3. Stolzoff, *The Good Enough Job*, 55.
4. Stolzoff, 182.
5. Lencioni, *The Advantage*, 27.
6. Lencioni, 48.
7. Durvasula, *It's Not You*, 42.
8. Durvasula, 83.
9. Durvasula, 42.
10. Durvasula, 47.
11. Fiore Higgins, *Bully Market*.
12. Stolzoff, *The Good Enough Job*, 13.

Chapter 9

13. Stolzoff, *The Good Enough Job*, 56.
14. Stolzoff, 78.
15. Chapman, et al., *Rising Above a Toxic Workplace*, 19.

16. Durvasula, *It's Not You*, 107.

17. Durvasula, 108.

18. Chapman, et al., 70–74.

19. Durvasula, *It's Not You*, 145.

20. Grabmeier, "Why Some Abusive Bosses Get a Pass from Their Employees."

21. Stolzoff, 182.

Chapter 12

22. Chapman, et al., 76.

23. Chapman, et al., 74.

24. Chapman, et al., 67.

25. Stolzoff, *The Good Enough Job*, 155.

References

Chapman, Gary, Paul White, and Harold Myra. *Rising Above a Toxic Workplace: Taking Care of Yourself in an Unhealthy Environment*. Northfield, 2014.

Durvasula, Ramani. *It's Not You: Identifying and Healing from Narcissistic People*. The Open Field, 2024.

Fiore Higgins, Jamie. *Bully Market: My Story of Money and Misogyny at Goldman Sachs*. Simon & Schuster, 2023.

Grabmeier, Jeff. "Why Some Abusive Bosses Get a Pass from Their Employees." www.news.osu.edu, July 8, 2022. Accessed September 17, 2024.

Lencioni, Patrick M. *The Advantage: Why Organizational Health Trumps Everything Else In Business*. 1st edition. San Francisco, Calif: Jossey-Bass, 2012.

Stolzoff, Simone. *The Good Enough Job: Reclaiming Life from Work*. Portfolio, 2023.

"Townhouse Notes: Toxic Work Environments: The History of an Idea | Perspectives on History | AHA." Accessed June 12, 2024.

"Toxic Workplace." *Wikipedia*, November 19, 2023. Accessed June 12, 2024.

Acknowledgements

To "Briana," "Evelyn," "Faith," "Nina," and "Miah," my deepest gratitude. Without your bravery, this book would not have been possible. Thank you for trusting me to tell your story.

To my classmates in the Soulful Nonfiction School and to Danielle Anderson with Ink Worthy Books, our soulful mentor. Danielle, you have created a space for stories to flourish and hearts to heal. Every one of us and our books benefited from your support, your tough love, and the multiple iterations of steps that seemed pointless in the moment! To my classmates, I can't wait to read all of your brilliant words. I'm so glad to know you.

To Kristin, my dear friend from the landing chats. Thank you for responding to my random reach out and for treating this special project with all of your brilliance, gentleness, kindness, and care. I am honored to call you friend, and this book would not be the same without you. In AOT, Wolfie.

To my family, friends, colleagues and coworkers past and present. Whether we speak regularly or have lost touch, thank you all for your role in making me who I am today. I wouldn't change a thing.

To Mel, thank you for supporting me through every toxic work experience, role-playing all the difficult conversations, and being my support through major life transitions. You are the reason I made it to the other side. Without you, this project would have died a thousand deaths. Thank you for your unwavering support, your gentle pushes (and occasional shove) when I needed a boost, and your never-ending kindness and care. I did this for us.

To the three Ts, thank you for your love and support. I know it's always there, even when it isn't obvious.

> "Mom's on the floor again."
> Sarcasm: It's how we hug.

About the Author

Susan Beth Cocuzza (Beth) is the Founder and Principal of Almavina Strategic Partners, LLC. She is an experienced leader, strategist, and advisor in the nonprofit sector. Passionate about organizational culture and effectiveness, Beth is equity-minded, mission-driven, and thrives on bringing order to chaos.

In 2023, a personal medical emergency led Beth to process the deep and lasting impact toxic work culture can have on mental, physical, and emotional health. Once the proverbial door was open, she started seeing it everywhere, and *Promises Broken* began to take shape. Now more than ever, Beth's work focuses on building strong organizational health through systemic change and leadership development.

Teetering on the edge of an empty nest, Beth currently lives in New Jersey with her husband and two sons. An avid reader, in her free time Beth can be found with a novel in her hands—preferably either wrapped in a blanket or sitting on the beach!

Beth can be found on Instagram at @almavinareads and LinkedIn at @beth-cocuzza. If you purchased this book online and are so inclined, a positive review would be most appreciated. Help spread the word about toxic work culture in mission-driven spaces!